CW01512684

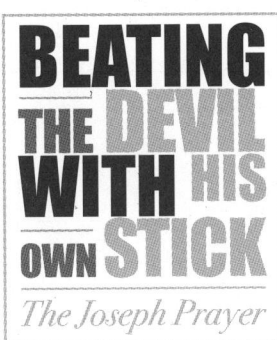

BEATING THE DEVIL WITH HIS OWN STICK

The Joseph Prayer

by Ray Sturdivant

MINING THE TRUTH PUBLISHING

Copyright © 2019 by Ray Sturdivant

All rights reserved under the international copyright law. No part of this book may be reproduced or transmitted in any form or by any means, electronic or mechanical, including photocopying, recording, or by any information storage and retrieval system, without the express, written permission of the author. The exception is reviewers, who may quote brief passages in a review.

ISBN 978-1-7336859-0-0
Mining the Truth Publishing
Dallas, TX

miningthetruth.com

Published by Mining the Truth
Dallas, TX

Printed in the United States of America

Unless otherwise indicated, Scriptures are taken from the NEW AMERICAN STANDARD BIBLE®, Copyright © 1960, 1962, 1963, 1968, 1971, 1972, 1973, 1975, 1977, 1995 by The Lockman Foundation. Used by permission.

Scriptures marked NIV are taken from THE HOLY BIBLE, NEW INTERNATIONAL VERSION®, NIV® Copyright © 1973, 1978, 1984, 2011 by Biblica, Inc.™ Used by permission. All rights reserved worldwide.

Scriptures marked NKJV are taken from the New King James Version. Copyright © 1982 by Thomas Nelson, Inc. Used by permission. All rights reserved.

Scriptures marked ESV are from The Holy Bible, English Standard Version® (ESV®), copyright © 2001 by Crossway, a publishing ministry of Good News Publishers. Used by permission. All rights reserved.

Book Cover Design by Ray Sturdivant

Endorsements:

Ray Sturdivant is a spiritual father to the community that I lead and pastor. He has prayed with hundreds of people resulting in true and lasting freedom. Beating The Devil With His Own Stick uncovers eight patterns common to all of us hindering us from experiencing the freedom Jesus has provided for us as His children. Ray's revelation is convicting, practical and deeply needed in our hour. Ray has mined the heart of both God and His people to uncover patterns impacting us from living in freedom and fullness of God's grace. This book will be a resource for the church in the days ahead. Thank you Ray and thank you Jesus.

—Michael Miller
Senior Pastor & Founder
Upper Room Dallas and Upper Room Global

Ray and I are good friends and I am thrilled to see Ray publish this book. From Bible studies to street ministry, we have been running together for many years. I respect Ray's passion for digging into the Word of God and his constant pursuit of the Lord in his own life.

The eight patterns Ray discusses in this book lend great insight into the amazing and unique plan that God has for our life as well as the strategies of the enemy that can keep us from fully walking out our calling. More than a method, the patterns Ray describes, are a framework for understanding God's plan for our lives which will produce fruit in your life in real-time as you read it.

In our ministry, as we began to understand these eight patterns, it helped us more effectively share the Gospel in the streets. It has also helped us unlock the God-given gifting, calling, and potential in our team members so that they are most effective in the calling they have on their life through our ministry.

This book will help reveal more of your God-given design, as well as the ability to see others through a new lens which will help you become more effective in your ministry to them.

—Kyle Martin
CEO/Founder,
Time to Revive

Ray Sturdivant is a man who fully understands that the weapons the enemy forms against us may be used against the devil and his minions for their detection, defeat and destruction. This book maps out a Biblical pathway for exposing the plans of the enemy and how to walk in God's Grace over your life. I encourage you to read "Beating the devil with his own stick—the Joseph's Prayer" with great expectation for personal insight and walking in victory.

—Rev. Paul N. E. Teske
Pastor, Mentor, Speaker
Author of Healing for Today

The names of the people in the stories you are about to encounter have been changed to protect the identity of those involved except in the cases where permission has been granted to use real names. Many times the Lord has told me, when someone encountered Him in a session with me, in the midst of their pit, that it was holy ground. On two occasions He had me remove my shoes in response. I did as I was told, wept and went to my knees. These stories are sacred testimonies of Jesus interacting with His bride to bring her back home. I don't share them as gossip or bragging rights but revelation and proof of the relentless love Jesus has for each one of us and the healing and freedom that abound as a result. May you handle them with the same sacred care they have been placed before you.

Contents

Grateful:

I am forever grateful to my wife Chrysty Sturdivant. She has been my biggest supporter, fan, and the love of my life. She is my partner in life and every spiritual advancement I have made has been a direct result of her being in my life. She has taught me how to more clearly communicate ideas that I assumed everyone would get just because they made sense to me.

I am thankful for everyone I have prayed with: I learned how precious we all are to Jesus by watching Him heal you.

And I am thankful to Jesus; you are everything to me. I am thankful to my best friend and co-author Holy Spirit. You make me look like I know what I am doing. And I am thankful to my Heavenly Father who rescued me out of darkness and put honor and meaning back in my heart for fatherhood.

Beginnings:

Answers to questions I didn't know to ask

Eight patterns that defined and changed me

By the time I woke up, God was already speaking to me. That morning I began to record the rapid-fire thoughts that flowed from His Spirit into my spirit and out onto the piece of paper right in front of me. I easily recognized the voice, since I communicate with Him on a regular, daily basis. I am an inner healing and deliverance prayer minister and I rely on the voice of God speaking to me and those I pray with to bring healing and deliverance. I know His voice; His voice is all I have.

This downpour came even though I had not yet been awake long enough to ask the questions He was answering. But I live in a place of questions. I try to keep my heart continuously postured like a satellite dish catching any heavenly signal coming my way. Believe me, questions had been asked—just not on that particular morning.

What He gave me, in an uninterrupted flow, were eight patterns common to everyone with whom I had ever prayed. As I examined the eight patterns, I realized, of the roughly 1,200 people I had prayed with up to that point, not one violated the eight patterns. Not that I could remember all of those people or their stories, but I couldn't recall any that contradicted the eight patterns, nor have the thousands I have prayed with since.

As this divine revelation hit my spirit, I was overwhelmed by the organized way in which He was summing up humanity's life experience right in front of me. I had always avoided the formulas that are found in many inner healing modalities, but what He was giving me was not a formula or way of doing ministry as much as a way of seeing or understanding. The reason I had never bought into formulas is that He never let me put Him in a box. Every time I thought I had Him in a predictable formula, He broke out of it.

I knew that what He was giving me that morning was not a mechanical formula to pray with but a way of seeing the deep inner workings of the human heart as it intersects with the goodness of God and the evil of our common enemy. These patterns offered an explanation like sitting beside Jesus in heaven and looking through a telescope at each person's life on planet Earth. They were heaven's view of the span of a human life summed up in eight patterns. Patterns are different from steps or formulas. God created seasons and times in the heavens and on earth to provide man with the necessary information to plan and to organize his activities around. They reveal to us where we are within a year or multiple years, which is especially important in an agricultural setting. Solomon tells us that, *"There is an appointed time for everything. A time to give birth and a time to die; A time to plant and a time to uproot what is planted. "—Ecclesiastes 3:1-2*

These eight patterns have become a lens that I can look through to give me a heavenly perspective on how Jesus is leading someone into freedom and intimacy with Him. But they are also a lens that I can invite the person I am praying with to look through so they can see the season they are in with Jesus, the enemy, and their destiny.

As all of this revelation was hitting my spirit, God then revealed to me that these same eight patterns were actually found in the story of Joseph. This realization wrecked me in a really good way. As I looked at the story of Joseph, I asked the Holy Spirit to show me the eight patterns. It was like He had the patterns on a transparency and laid them over the story. I was stunned as I realized that these eight patterns applied not only to Joseph but also to everyone who had ever lived. I suddenly knew it was the reason the Joseph story is so universally loved. Joseph's story is everyone's story. It's the story of God declaring gifting, destiny and purpose and the enemy attacking that very purpose. It's the story of God redeeming every attack by fulfilling the destiny of anyone with a willing, surrendered heart.

I wept as I saw the goodness of God on a heart level that I had never seen or felt before. This was not more left brain information; this was Spirit to spirit communication straight from the author of all truth. He was writing on my heart what He intended to come out of me and into other hearts, and eventually onto pages of paper to touch a bigger audience than I could ever possibly pray with.

The goodness of God wasn't on display to me solely because He redeems the attacks of the enemy. What He showed me, that morning, was that He actually takes THE exact attack of the enemy and uses that very thing to defeat the devil and tell our story. God took Joseph's rejection and slavery in Egypt and used it as the low point on the divine trampoline that elevated Him to become the leader of Egypt, and second only to Pharaoh. In other words, God loves to beat the devil with his own stick.

What He gave me that morning were eight keys to the universal questions philosophers, poets, pastors, and priests have been asking since the beginning of time about why bad things happen to good people. Does God cause or co-author evil by allowing it? I had already been learning for some time from Him that you will never be truly free until you allow Him to answer those questions in your own heart. I don't believe the answers are attainable on your own. Without His perspective, we are stuck running on the ever-expanding circular track of human reasoning. I have discovered as I pray with others that God can answer in five minutes questions that have taken a lifetime to ask. I have also found the real answers are received in our hearts and not just our heads.

This revelation has become an organized way to help speed up the discovery process for the person I am praying with as they find, through the laboratory of their own lives, the answers that bring healing, peace, and freedom. I have watched God answer these seemingly unanswerable questions directly as He interacts with the person I am praying with through visions, thoughts and heart encounters. He is the only One who honestly has the right to answer these questions.

What He has given me has changed my life, and the lives of those I pray with because it has changed the way I see. On the following pages are the eight patterns He has given you and I through the story of Joseph.

I now see my life and purpose through the eyes of a Father who absolutely loves me and Who is more than willing to pour out the resources of heaven on my behalf when I surrender. It has also changed the lives of those I pray with for the exact same reason. My prayer is that you will let Him bring heaven's perspective to your interpretation of your own story and to the stories of those you encounter.

It is the only story that matters; it is the story of God's redemption. It is the story of Joseph, and it is my story. My prayer is you will see that it is your story too.

Pattern 1:

God speaks before our heart beats

*He prophesies gifting and destiny over us in the womb
and into the spiritual realm*

Joseph's Pattern 1: God breathes life into each one of us in our mother's womb. What you may not realize is that scripture also tells us, according to Psalm 139:16, that God prophesies over each one of us in the womb, our destiny, gifting, and call. Even though, after we are born we have no memory of that heavenly encounter, it still gets planted deep in our heart as desire. God wants to give us the desires of our heart that He actually put there. For that to happen, the prophetic desires have to manifest in some way in our life so that we can partner with God and know how and what to pursue.

How Joseph's womb prophecy manifested in his life was through two God-given dreams. The two dreams revealed that he would be a world leader to the point that even his family would submit to his authority. He also demonstrated the gift of dream interpretation with his own dreams, and with the dreams of others while in Egypt. An anointing of wisdom and leadership also became evident to everyone he came into contact with in Egypt. Every one of the gifts God prophesied about Joseph in the womb started functioning as he stepped into his destiny in Egypt.

Then Joseph had a dream, and when he told it to his brothers, they hated him even more. He said to them, "Please listen to this dream which I have had; for behold, we were binding sheaves in the field, and lo, my sheaf rose up and also stood erect; and behold, your sheaves gathered around and bowed down to my sheaf..."

Now he had still another dream, and related it to his brothers, and said, "Lo, I have had still another dream; and behold, the sun and the moon and eleven stars were bowing down to me." — Genesis 37:5-7, 9

Joseph's prophetic truth: You are a world leader, and dream interpreter with the gifts of wisdom and leadership.

The idea of God prophesying over us while in the incubator of our mother's womb was a spiritual reality that hit my heart with awe and wonder the day the Holy Spirit revealed it to me. The answer came as a response to questions raised as a result of recognizing people's gifting by the way the enemy was attacking their lives. It didn't make sense to me because the demonic realm and Satan do not have access to the Holy Spirit, and as far as I knew, they could not see the future. So my question, which God answered that day, was; How does the enemy see a person's gifting even before that person is saved? How could they possibly know, long before the person does, their gifting and destiny? Frequently, God revealed to me the demonic tactic of attacking people's gifting and destiny some time before age seven. Occasionally, the attacks started even as early as the womb.

Inner healing, deliverance, and definitions

All of this insight came about as a result of being a full-time prayer minister. To explain what I do, I use the terms inner healing/ deliverance throughout this book. The following words explain inner healing/deliverance which will be greatly expanded upon as we go on this journey of the story of Joseph together. I define the term inner healing as the process of leading a person to an intimate encounter with Jesus, where He heals the heart of soul wounds and traumatic events and displaces lie-based-pain with His truth. I define deliverance as the process of breaking the power of demonic strongholds in a person's life through repentance and commanding the demons involved to leave through the authority of Jesus and the power of the Holy Spirit. A typical prayer session that I lead lasts two hours and includes both inner healing and deliverance.

Words of the womb

While ministering to others through these two-hour sessions, I started noticing the enemy's pattern of attacking their gifting before they even knew Jesus. This caused me to ask the questions He ultimately answered. God spoke the first answer to me by saying that He prophesies over everyone—their gifting, destiny, and call—while they are in the womb. As I sat in silence, exploring the significance of what I just heard, I began wondering if I understood correctly. That's when He brought to my mind verses backing up what He just spoke to my spirit.

Your eyes have seen my unformed substance; (An embryo in my mother's womb)
and in your book were all written
the days that were ordained
when as yet there was not one of them. (Gifting, destiny, and call)
— Psalm 139:16

He continued to prove His point by showing me in the book of Jeremiah what He said to Jeremiah in chapter 1 verse 5: *"Before I formed you in the womb I knew you, And before you were born I consecrated you; I have appointed you a prophet to the nations."* In the book of Isaiah, He said to Isaiah twice, "I called you from your mother's womb to be a prophet to Israel." Paul said in the book of Galatians; *"But when God, who had set me apart even from my mother's womb and called me through His grace, was pleased to reveal His Son in me so that I might preach Him among the Gentiles."* He then took me to the order of creation in Genesis and showed me seven times He spoke something into existence, "Let there be light... Let Us make man in Our own image."... He revealed to me that He creates by speaking things into existence.

"God, who gives life to the dead and calls into being that which does not exist."
—Romans 4:17b

Prophecy is not passive

When He prophesies about an event, it will happen— you can bank on it. When He prophesies about an individual life, that person will have to align him or herself with the prophecy before it is fulfilled. His words create possibilities that didn't exist one-second before He spoke, but He requires human agreement to make that prophetic possibility manifest as a reality in life. The Bible is full of examples of people falling short of everything God had for them because of a lack of agreement on their part.

"Samuel said to Saul, 'You have acted foolishly; you have not kept the commandment of the Lord your God, which He commanded you, for now the Lord would have established your kingdom over Israel forever. But now your kingdom shall not endure.'" —1 Samuel 13:13-14b

The answer He gave me that day revealed the first of the eight patterns that I since learned were common to everyone I have ever or ever would pray with. That morning, I gained an understanding that when God speaks over us in the womb, His words land in our heart and attract us to our call, gifting, and destiny like a GPS tracking device. The only problem is that those same words draw the attention of the demonic realm because His prophetic words go out into the entire spiritual realm. This truth implies that the enemy hears the words and then knows precisely what to attack. This is how he knows what to make a pre-emptive strike against to try and thwart the plans that God has for each one of us to impact His kingdom.

Mining for gold

This explains our emotional response when we receive accurate prophetic words. Many times our knees buckle and eyes water because exact prophetic words reconnect our heart to what God already prophesied over us in the womb. Prophetic words realign our hearts with heaven's intention for our lives, intentions that have been there not only from the womb but before the act of creation itself *(Eph. 1:4)*. We were birthed out of the heart of the Father an eternity before we were ever birthed out of the wombs of our mothers. Just like gold deposits placed beneath the earth's surface, God placed a rich deposit of Jesus in our heart in the form of the prophetic words He spoke over us in the womb. They lay there like gold, undetected until we mine for truth and find Jesus. He leads us right to that vein of pure gold buried deep in our hearts that bear witness of Him.

"But we have this treasure in earthen vessels, so that the surpassing greatness of the power will be of God and not from ourselves." —2 Corinthians 4:7

Satan hates you

The enemy's intentions for us couldn't be in further opposition to God's. The enemy's hatred of God doesn't compare to his hatred of the image bearers of God. Since you and I are much easier targets than God and we seem totally inferior to Satan, we bear the full weight of the wrath of Satan. He and the demonic realm are in a rage because of their impotence in seizing the throne of God by force *(Isa. 14:12- 15)*. So they aim every one of their laser-guided missiles of evil against the image bearers of God who were created to rule the very planet Satan lost to Jesus on the battleground of Calvary's hill. Jesus describes the contrast between His plan for each of us and Satan's plan in the following passage:

"The thief comes only to steal and kill and destroy; I came that they may have life, and have it abundantly." — John 10:10

A heart tuned to heaven's song

God aims every one of His love missiles at the heart aligned with heaven, and abundant life flows as a result. When that happens, prophetic words put on skin and bones and run the race without encumbrance that He sang over us in the womb. When our heart aligns with the song of heaven, all the resources of heaven are sent to silence the agents of hell before they can silence the song we were created to sing.

Old stories, new truths

We know from the Apostle Paul that the Old Testament was written to teach us spiritual realities from the real-life examples of the stories told in those ancient books *(1 Cor. 10:1-11)*. We can conclude from these Biblical stories that very few of us will ever live out the fullness of our destinies, as God intended. Very few of the Hebrews even entered the promised land, let alone occupied every part that God had given them.

The promised land is an Old Testament revelation of the spiritual destiny or inheritance that God has for each of us under the New Covenant. We hear the voice of God speaking to us today, as He did to Joshua, when he told him to be strong and courageous before he crossed over the Jordan to lead the Israelites into the promised land. We can obey the same words and inherit the land of our destiny and promise in the spiritual realm that has real-life consequences. He also promises to us, just like He promised Joshua—that He had given him the whole land but only where his foot tread would he experience it. In other words, He tells us today that all of the enemies of our destiny have already been defeated. And just like He said to Joshua, only in the areas we are willing to show up and possess will we receive that part of our land. Jesus has already won the battle for us, but we can forfeit it as easily as the Hebrews.

Joseph fits the pattern

The next revelation that these eight patterns actually tell the story of Joseph hit me just as hard. As I examined the story of Joseph, God showed me the patterns in his life as if He held them on a transparent sheet over the Biblical text. Staring at me in unarguable order was the Joseph story as if it were written to specifically follow the eight patterns.

As I looked at how this first pattern related to the Joseph story, I realized that his two prophetic dreams revealed what God had prophesied over him in the womb. The prophecy God sings over each one of us has to somehow manifest in our lives after we are born, so that we recognize our destiny and gifting to live it out fully. That was the purpose of the two dreams of Joseph. They revealed what God had already put in his heart in the womb. It seems that Joseph's father Jacob knew there was a unique, God-given, destiny on Joseph's life that was very powerful.

A colorful coat paints a big picture

That idea explains one of the reasons why Joseph was Jacob's favorite. Without Jacob fully recognizing the significance of it, he gave Joseph a multi-colored tunic. That robe was longer than customary for that period and was a prophetic picture of the royal office Joseph would one day occupy in Egypt. The multiple colors of the tunic appear to represent the multitude of races and people he would rule over. It was also a picture of the fulfillment of God's promise to Abraham to be a father of many nations which also implies multiple colors of people.

Big dreams

The first dream about the sheaves of wheat was an indication of how powerful Joseph was going to be; even his brothers were going to bow down in submission to his authority. I also find it interesting that the symbolism used was wheat. I believe this part of the dream pictured why the brothers were going to submit. They would one day have to come to Egypt to get grain from Joseph to survive the coming famine. In other words, their collective ability to gather food would fail as Joseph's divinely empowered ability to provide would eventually feed his whole family.

The second dream expands on the revelation and includes his parents, represented as the sun and moon, and the brothers as the eleven stars. Frequently in scripture astrological symbols represent spiritual powers. Throughout the Bible, stars represent both good and bad angels. In ancient Egypt, the sun god "Ra" was the dominant figure among the high gods and retained this position from early in that civilization's history. Khonsu was an ancient Egyptian god of the moon since the earliest times in Egyptian mythology.

The Holy Spirit showed me that this second dream not only pictures the whole family submitting to Joseph's authority, but also pictures the power Joseph carried in the spiritual realm. God was prophesying in that dream what He had prophesied over him in the womb. He was going to force all of the soldiers of darkness to bow before the reign and rule of Joseph in Egypt which was ground zero of Satan's domination of the Earth at that time.

Spiritual jiu-jitsu

The spiritual temper tantrum the enemy launched against Joseph as a result of this revelation was countered in force by God. He redeemed every attack to make Joseph the most powerful man on earth in his day, and he made Satan and the entire demonic realm bow before him. God is a master of spiritual jiu-jitsu, turning the strength of His opponent against Him. Even though Pharaoh retained his title and status, for all practical purposes, he turned rulership over to Joseph. Pharaoh was Satan's power on earth at the time, and even he submitted to the authority and anointing of heaven that was on Joseph.

"Moreover, Pharaoh said to Joseph, Though I am Pharaoh, yet without your permission no one shall raise his hand or foot in all the land of Egypt." — *Genesis 41:44*

Raised up to rule

You and I were created to rule our God-given version of Egypt. When our hearts align with the intention of heaven, even the demonic realm must submit to us the same way it did to Joseph and to the 70 that Jesus sent out in Luke 10. They came back fired up and said: "Lord, even the demons are subject to us in your name." When this alignment happens, Joseph's story becomes our story. Jesus died to help us accomplish our part in securing His kingdom on earth just like

He did with Joseph. Along with that Kingdom purpose comes great blessing, anointing, and power in the spirit realm.

We become part of the fulfillment of the prophecy against Satan in Genesis 3:15. In this passage, God cursed the serpent, as the agent used by Satan, for his role in the fall of Adam and Eve. At the same time, He prophesied about the coming of Jesus and the ultimate defeat of Satan which we take part in when we come into alignment with the Words of the womb over our lives.

And I will put enmity
Between you and the woman,
And between your seed and her seed;
He shall bruise you on the head,
And you shall bruise him on the heel."
— *Genesis 3:15*

Step on the snake

A close look at the original Hebrew reveals that this passage can be translated as follows: He shall crush your head, and you shall bruise His heel. This way of viewing the passage really speaks to my heart about what I see as being prophesied. The crushing of the head is the defeat of Satan at the cross which is the same place as the bruising of Jesus' heel. Bruising is painful but not fatal. This is a picture of the nonfatal (heel) wound of the cross because Jesus resurrected stronger than before His death. Crushing a snake's head is the most effective way to kill it. The head is Satan's favorite place to attack humanity. Most of the warfare we experience in this life occurs on the battlefield of our minds.

Given that we are Jesus' literal body on earth, when you and I partner with God by operating out of peace and love, God uses our feet to enforce the crushing of the head of the serpent Satan. Romans 16:20 echoes this sentiment: *"The God of all peace will soon crush Satan under your feet."*

One day, the defeat of Satan will get enforced to the point that he will be bound for a thousand years when Jesus returns to earth to set up His earthly kingdom. After that time, the ultimate enforcement will occur when Satan and his demons are confined to Hell for all of eternity. Until then, the body of Christ is involved in an aggressive, spiritual, advancement of His kingdom throughout the Earth.

Ours, however, is not a military mission, but a spiritual one. Every time we lead someone to Jesus, deliver someone from affliction, oppression, addiction, or infirmity, or disciple them, etc., we advance the kingdom of God on Earth, and the crushing of Satan continues under our feet.

Each one of us accomplishes this by discovering the gifting, destiny, and call that God has breathed over each one of us and then relentlessly walking it out. When we do, we reclaim the Kingdom of God one person at a time. We become heaven's partner to bring the Kingdom of God to Earth. We fulfill the mandate God originally gave Adam and Eve to fill the Earth, subdue it, and rule over it. *(Gen. 1:28)*

Jesus speaks Vicki's language

One of the tools God has given me to use during inner healing I call; "Words of the womb." I lead the person I am praying with to ask God to let them hear what He spoke over them in the womb. It is a powerful way to discover gifting, destiny, and call. An example of this tool happened when I prayed with Vicki. During the opening prayer, I started getting prophetic words for her from the Holy Spirit. He spoke through me that she would move in the prophetic in such a powerful way that she would be called a prophetess. So not only would she be prophetic, but also she would be promoted to the office of prophet.

He also called out the fact that she had a mercy gift and that it would always temper the prophetic words she got in order to speak the love of Jesus into those she would prophesy to. She was also called into a Song of Solomon type intimacy with Jesus that would flow out of her to those she encountered. He continued to speak through me that as she received healing, her heart would become so tightly knit with Jesus that she would carry His love for His body into every encounter and that love would heal wounded hearts.

That's how we started her powerful session. Toward the end of her session, I led her to ask Jesus to speak what was prophesied over her in the womb. He gave her the following words; I tried my best to capture them as the words came out of her faster than I could write them down.

"I placed you as a prophetess over the nations, to call forth my children back to my heart, To restore my relationship with them as a Father, how a father looks at a child, To bind up the brokenhearted, restore the wounded, To bring redemption to my children. You are so special to me my darling. I will use your voice to bring healing, to call forth those in mourning, To rejoice with dancing. I will use you to help those get up who cannot walk. I filled you to overflow and anoint those to come into ministry. Your hands have been anointed since birth to bring healing, prophecy, and anointing to bind up wounds. Your hug will comfort many that mourn, many that are in pain. You are a touch of the Father's heart."

I will never forget that session, and neither will she. It's one thing to get a prophetic word from a well-known prophet; it is quite another to get those words from Jesus directly. Receiving from Him, the words that were spoken over you in the womb will radically change your life as it reconnects your heart back to His.

14-year-old heart surgeon

An incident that radically reconnected my heart to Jesus happened at a conference. There was a well-known speaker at a conference I attended and I wanted to receive prayer from him so that God might impart gifts to me through the prayer. The Biblical concept of impartation has many examples of God releasing gifts through the laying on of hands. Elijah passed on a double portion of his spirit through the laying of hands on Elisha. Paul imparted spiritual gifts to Timothy through the laying on of hands and prayer.

If I'm honest, I had the desire for impartation a little out of whack. God revealed this to me in a humorous and humbling way. At that conference, the well-known person laid hands on me, and I was very powerfully touched by God, but he did not speak or pray any prophetic words over me. I thought I needed those words to function in all that God had for me. I left the auditorium after the encounter to go to lunch, and I was bummed. At that moment, I heard the Holy Spirit say to me, "Do you think he is the only way I can impart the gifts you need?" Immediately I heard a little girl of about 14 running up to me and yelling, "Mister." I turned around, and she said: "I see the power of God all over you, and you are going to be very important in the Kingdom."

Those little girl's words cut deep into my heart and found the tender wounded part, and they made me weep. My grown man tears may have been a little too much for her because she looked at my response and ran out the door before I could tell her the powerful way in which God had just used her. God used a little girl to realign my heart to heaven's intention for my life. At the same time, He was giving me a big smile saying, "Knock it off. You have the big names and the gifts a little out of whack right now. I will give you the desires of your heart because I placed them there, but I have to keep your connection to me greater than the gifts I give, or they will destroy you." Our heart has to always be expanding larger than our gifts.

Lies pollute purpose

It is hard to imagine how we let the enemy create such a distorted view of God in us that we believe we have no purpose. Even an ant has a purpose in God's creation. Everything in creation has a specific purpose in the overall function of the planet. How much more purpose, gifting, and plan must His image bearers carry?

Jesus frequently uses the natural realm to teach us spiritual realities, and even a brief glance at creation reveals a creator with brilliant design and purpose. Even the most mundane of creatures have extravagant detail of design and purpose. I love to look at a shadow box that my friend Lana has of various butterflies from all over the world pinned to a board in the framed box. The color, detail, and design of each butterfly will make you gasp if you care to look close enough. Art always reflects the heart of the creator. All of creation reveals the extravagant heart of the creative God we love and surrender to.

Lana's lament

Lana has fantastic taste and artistic expression in everything in her life, from the way she dresses to the way she decorates her house. Everything she touches becomes another artful expression of her heart. You would think the clear articulation of herself through her artistic taste and expression would have a bold, confident soul behind it. To prove the enemy never sleeps, he had attacked her so repeatedly through people and circumstances that she thought her unique expressions were what caused people to reject her. The enemy tried to pervert a unique God-given trait of hers into a form of rebellion and self-protection. All in anticipation of rejection from others, which she was sure would come her way. Even though she loved art and color and all the artistic ways she looked at life, she never felt like she had God's stamp of approval on the way she expressed herself.

The Holy Spirit gave me a vision, and a word for her that I think expresses God's passionate desire for us to be conformed to the image of Jesus, while being a unique expression of God's creation. He showed me a picture of His hand with a glove on it, and the glove looked exactly like Lana had made it and decorated it. It just seemed like her taste. It was very colorful with wild designs and rhinestones all over it. I then shared the revelation that we are all gloves on the hand of Jesus. He empowers our movement, agility, power, and purpose but we are the visible manifestation of His unique expression of Himself to the world. As I began to describe to her the glove that represented her, it brought her great joy that her love for art actually came from the hand of Jesus.

You're His piece of work

I can say the same thing about you. The gifts, calling and destiny on your life are as unique to you as your physical DNA or your fingerprint. Nobody like you has ever existed or ever will exist again. You are the glove on Jesus' hand that is His unique expression to the world. You are the glove that He wants to touch your world through. According to Ephesians 2, you are his masterpiece. The Greek word "poíēma" translates in the verse as masterpiece or workmanship. It is where we get the word poem from. You are His poem that He is writing with your life, and He wants the world to read it. To Him, you are a unique work of art with a very unique purpose and place in His kingdom.

It's your identity as a son or daughter of Jesus. Your identity is who you are. It's where you fit in and where you belong in the Kingdom. You have a unique assignment in the Kingdom sculpted just for you. Your Father has a place for you in His house. Your destiny, call, and gifts all come together to form your identity.

Your name is part of your identity and means a lot more than we recognize today culturally. Names in the West today don't mean what they did in Biblical times. In Biblical times and in other cultures today, names have meaning. In Biblical times the names were very prophetic descriptions of the person in terms of the kind of person they were going to be and many times even described their character. God frequently changed the names of people after they had a significant encounter with Him.

Knowing Him is a name changer

He changed the name of Jacob (supplanter or schemer) to Israel (God prevails) after wrestling with Jesus all night for the blessing he had schemed his whole life to get *(Gen. 32:28)*. God changed the name of Saul to Paul after the power of God knocked him off his donkey, and he came to know Jesus. He changed Simon's name to Peter after a significant encounter with Jesus. The fact that He has a pet name for you that only you and He know shows the intimate connection Jesus has with your identity.

You have a name written in heaven if you trust in Jesus. But there is a unique name reserved for those who are overcomers written in Heaven. In Revelation 2 Jesus says that He will give to him who overcomes a white stone with a new name written on the stone which no one knows but he who receives it. What is not clear is when the name is revealed. We don't receive the white stone until we get to heaven, but the pet name could quite possibly be revealed while on earth as we draw closer to Him and overcome the attacks of the enemy while on this Earth. That identity will represent who you are to Him for all of eternity. It will express the intimate connection with Jesus that overcoming the enemy requires. It will represent a spiritual upgrade like the name changes given in the Biblical examples. That name will relate to what was prophesied over you in the womb and to your calling, gifting, and destiny here on Earth.

Receiving value releases identity

The key to maximizing the benefit of knowing your true identity is not to get your value from it. In pattern eight, we will take a deeper dive into the importance of separating value from identity. Value is the price that love is willing to pay for you, and identity is who He says you are. It is your gifting, destiny, and calling in your life.

We abuse our identity when we try to use it to increase our value in the eyes of the world and God. That is not the purpose of identity. Its purpose is to show you that you belong and where you fit in the Kingdom. Identity provides the reassurance that you have a place in your Father's house, and that can be a life-changing discovery for anyone who has experienced a lifetime of rejection. The more you walk in your true identity, the more the world will reject you, and the more your value will have to be a settled issue in your heart.

Without living out of your true identity or true self (your spirit), you will be forced to try to find your identity in the world. This activity will become the chains that bind your heart to this Earth. Identity is such a key component to living in freedom and the abundant life Jesus promised. But it is not the most important thing. The most important thing is knowing and receiving your value. Knowing you are loved eternally and unconditionally has to come before you can walk in freedom in your destiny, purpose, and gifting.

Identity comes to us from the Father. Your name represents your identity. You are defined by coming from the Father and by knowing Him and being known by Him. This is made clear in the first line of Paul's prayer for the Ephesians found in chapter 3.

"For this reason, I bow my knees before the Father, from whom every family in heaven and on earth derives its name."
—*Ephesians 3:14*

No one like you exists

When we grasp the uniqueness of our identity, we recognize the futility of comparing ourselves with others. No one like you has ever existed or will ever exist again, so who are you going to compare yourself to? If you compare yourself to someone else, you will always come up short because you were never meant to be them. If you come up superior, you were using a false standard of comparison. There is no way you can be superior to them because you don't have the resources and anointing of heaven to be them. A foot can't say to the eye, "I make a better eye than you." An eye cannot say to the foot, "I have no need of you," because an eye cannot walk. Paul says something very similar to this in 1 Corinthians 12.

God in your face

If you allow it, a very intimate picture will come to your mind of God knitting us, forming us, prophesying over us, and breathing life into us as in the womb. And by the way, scripture confirms this activity of God on our behalf. David, the man after God's own heart, called this activity meditating on scripture. This mental imagery is also how Daniel described visions. He called them visions in the mind. Mental pictures can be simple still images that last for a second or a big screen TV dropping down from heaven with full color and motion that you see with both eyes open and everything in between. Visions are a powerful way to have encounters with God and His words, which will seal your identity in Him.

This intimate picture of the Father's activity in the womb is the way that we all start life, regardless of what our circumstances are in the natural realm. Our ultimate journey after we are born is to regain that intimate connection with the Father that started at the moment of conception. If our lives are ever going to be complete, we are to live out the gifting, and destiny He prophesied over us in the womb by living out of our true identity as the original self He created in the womb.

Gospel sparks start fires

Regaining that connection has a starting point as distinct as when the power and light of heaven knocked Saul of Tarsus to the ground, and he stood up 3 days later as Paul the Apostle *(Acts 9:3-19)*. That starting point for Paul and us is Jesus, and the entry point is the gospel. There has been a battle over what the gospel is for almost 2,000 years. What challenges us about the gospel is that it's a heart issue. And the heart of the gospel is Jesus. It's all about Him. It's knowing Him and being known by Him.

Right from the beginning

The Holy Spirit, on occasion, has me address the gospel in sessions because it is so foundational to freedom and therefore everything built on top of it. This makes the gospel as the foundation a critical issue. Many people need deliverance and inner healing because they don't have a heart revelation that they are saved by grace and not by their works. On a heart level, they are stuck like hamsters in a wheel of human performance trying to appease what they perceive as an angry God. The gospel is based on grace.

"For by grace you have been saved through faith; and that not of yourselves, it is the gift of God; not as a result of works, so that no one may boast." — *Ephesians 2:8-9*

It's not about you

The gospel is not based on how good you are, it is based on how good Jesus is on your behalf.

"For not knowing about God's righteousness and seeking to establish their own, they did not subject themselves to the righteousness of God. For Christ is the end of the law for righteousness to everyone who believes." —Romans 10:3-4

Jesus is the Rock portrayed in this scripture and throughout scripture. *"And the rain fell, and the floods came, and the winds blew and slammed against that house; and yet it did not fall, for it had been founded on the rock."* — *Matthew 7:25*

The sand, in the analogy, represents human ability or works. *"Everyone who hears these words of Mine and does not act on them, will be like a foolish man who built his house on the sand. The rain fell, and the floods came, and the winds blew and slammed against that house; and it fell—and great was its fall." —Matthew 7:26-27*

It's about Him

The gospel is receiving Jesus. It's standing on Jesus, the Rock, and not standing on your ability to perform or be righteous, the sand.

If we understand how we are saved, it will produce stability, security, and freedom in Jesus. The focus of the gospel is Jesus. The content of the gospel is found in 1 Corinthians 15:1-4. The apostle Paul should know what the gospel is since he wrote 1/3 of the New Testament. As we look at this scripture, I am going to ask you to hit the pause button on the part of verse 2 that says, Unless you believed in vain. We will deal with that in just a minute. Paul says that what he is about to give is the gospel and he states that fact four different ways.

1.) *I make known to you the gospel which I preached*

2.) *Which also you received*

3.) *In which also you stand*

4.) *By which also you are saved*

You have to agree with Paul that what we are about to read is the gospel. *"Now I make known to you, brethren, the gospel which I preached to you, which also you received, in which also you stand, by which also you are saved, if you hold fast the word which I preached to you, unless you believed in vain. For I delivered to you as of first importance what I also received, that Christ died for our sins according to the Scriptures, and that He was buried, and that He was raised on the third day according to the Scriptures."* —1 Corinthians 15:1-4

According to this passage, there are three things a person has to receive in his or her heart about Jesus to be in eternal relationship with Him.

*1. **Jesus died for our sins**,* according to the Scriptures

*2. **He was buried** (proof of death).*

*3. **He was raised on the third day according to the Scriptures.***

As we drop down to verse 12 in the same chapter, we will deal with what it means to believe in vain.

"Now if Christ is preached, that He has been raised from the dead, how do some among you say that there is no resurrection of the dead? But if there is no resurrection of the dead, not even Christ has been raised; and if Christ has not been raised, then our preaching is vain, your faith also is vain." —1 Corinthians 15:12-14

Believing in vain, according to Paul, amounts to claiming to believe in Jesus and, at the same time, denying that he was raised from the dead.

In other words, there were those Paul was addressing that denied the resurrection, but still claimed to believe in Jesus. That is not faith at all, but a vain faith because it denies half of the gospel and the very means of salvation. According to the Apostle Paul, if you have received the death, burial, and resurrection of Jesus into your heart, then you are saved and cannot ever be separated from God.

It's a heart issue

The gospel is not intellectually agreeing to some facts on a page, so you get to go to heaven one day. The gospel is surrendering your religious striving to be good enough for God to accept you and receiving Jesus. It's receiving all of Him, His works, His Lordship, and His divine and human nature. It's surrendering your heart and life to King Jesus.

You are no longer on the throne, and neither is anyone else except Jesus. That surrender releases an empowering grace to live a life that was impossible without Him. And yes, as a result, you will spend all eternity with Him, but you will already have eternity in your heart from the moment you believe. You will be a new empowered creation that didn't exist one second before you received Him. All of your sin and even the source of your sin will be permanently wiped out as we cover in Pattern 6. You will have gone from spiritual death to life. You will be transferred from the kingdom of darkness to the kingdom of light. Don't get caught up in the intellectual debate and over-analysis of salvation. It's a simple entry point of receiving Jesus. If you have Jesus, you have salvation, healing, and deliverance. You have life, and you have rest. You have everything. Now the words He spoke over you in the womb can be grabbed hold of and lived out.

Who God is to us in Pattern 1: Elohim = The Creator God

Elohim expresses the part of God's identity that speaks and causes universes to explode into existence. It's the plural form of a word that reveals there are three personalities engaged in the Genesis story. It's the expression of the intimate part of His heart that shaped dirt into human form with just a thought. Dirt took form, moistened with His life-giving breath, released through mouth-to-mouth contact with Adam. God kissed his lips, and breath entered Adam's lungs, causing him to stand upright and reflect back to God His very image.

It's the part of Him that recreates the Genesis story in the fertile soil of our mother's womb as He gets close enough to breathe life, purpose, destiny, and gifting into each one of us. With each breath on a womb, He causes another birth of a unique expression of Him never before seen. Without a deep connection to the words prophesied over us in the womb by Elohim, we will aimlessly wander this planet asking the same old questions that prophets, poets, and philosophers have wasted their lives on, looking for answers that can only be found in Him. Connect intimately with Elohim and His words, and you will know who you are and why you were created. Then your life will align with every breath He exhales in your direction, causing your entire being and life to expand with the fullness of Him. In short, you will know and be known, and that will change you, and everything Elohim breathes on through you.

Scripture: Your eyes have seen my unformed substance;
and in your book were all written
the days that were ordained
when as yet there was not one of them. — *Psalm 139:16*

Tool: Words of the womb

Activation:
- Ask the Father to reveal everything He prophesied over you in the womb.

- Make sure you write it down and speak it out loud over your life on a regular basis.
- Come into agreement with the prophetic words of your Creator and they will come to pass.

Pattern 2:

Satan plants lies in pain

The enemy attacks our identity, destiny, and gifts
with wounds, lies, and generational iniquity.

Joseph's Pattern 2: The enemy poked a hole in Joseph's heart and planted the seed of rejection right in the middle of it. Rejection of his destiny came through his parents. His brothers not only rejected him, his destiny, and his gifts but actually sold him into slavery in Egypt. This pre-emptive strike by the enemy against Joseph's role in the kingdom of God was so targeted that it came with specificity after his gifts and destiny. His destiny was to be a world leader, and the opposite of a world leader is a slave. And slavery is precisely what the enemy, through his brothers, sold him into.

"Then his brothers said to him, 'Are you actually going to reign over us? Or are you really going to rule over us?' So they hated him even more for his dreams and for his words."…

"He related it to his father and to his brothers; and his father rebuked him and said to him, 'What is this dream that you have had? Shall I and your mother and your brothers actually come to bow ourselves down before you to the ground?'"…

"So it came about, when Joseph reached his brothers, that they stripped Joseph of his tunic, the varicolored tunic that was on him; and they took him and threw him into the pit. Now the pit was empty, without any water in it."...

"Then some Midianite traders passed by, so they pulled him up and lifted Joseph out of the pit, and sold him to the Ishmaelites for twenty shekels of silver. Thus they brought Joseph into Egypt." — *Genesis 37:8, 10, 23-24, 28*

Joseph's soul wounds: Rejection, abandonment, violence, and humiliation followed Joseph right up to Pattern 6, when unconditional surrender changed everything.

Joseph's probable core lie: Your life doesn't matter.

The fact that Satan attacks us won't come as a news flash to anyone who has walked with Jesus for any length of time. But his attack aimed specifically at our gifts, destiny, and call starting at an early age, was certainly a surprise to me. As I mentioned in the previous chapter, it was stunning to be able to recognize what a person's gifting was by the targeted way the enemy attacked his/her life. I discovered that one of the main assaults frequently comes in the form of a core lie jabbed into the heart at an early age by the demonic realm. Like quills on a porcupine, this barbed lie works its way in deeper and deeper as we squirm under the painful effects of every devaluing word and event.

You're looking through a lens

The core lie operates as the distorted lens we look through to interpret every circumstance of our lives from the time it enters our lives. It continues until the time it gets displaced with the truth of the value the Father has placed on our lives. Core lies are specific, devaluing lies about us and are "I am" statements such as: "I'm not good enough," "I'm unworthy," "I'm useless," etc. Any statements about others are not core lies. It might be a lie, but it is not a core lie unless it is a devaluing lie about the person. "My father doesn't love me," is not a core lie. Lies about others are frequently just splinter lies off the core lie because the core lie not only distorts how we see ourselves, but also how we see others. We cannot honestly assess the actions and motivations of ourselves or others while looking through the distorted lens of a core lie.

It's been there all along

Out of the thousands of people I have prayed with, I have seen core lies enter someone's heart, almost exclusively, at six years old or younger. Only two have entered at age seven. The wickedness of our enemy is revealed, in the fact that the first seven years of life are the most formative years for brain development of a child. The brain develops more and faster during these years than any other time in life and is at its most vulnerable state. The fact that he goes after children with deep emotional pain, infecting them with core lies during these formative years, reveals a very targeted strategy to wound with maximum effect. This forces us all to recognize the genuine evil we are up against, and also explains why Jesus had such a sincere desire for children to attach to Him early. He knows our enemy well. *"But Jesus called for them, saying, "Permit the children to come to Me, and do not hinder them, for the kingdom of God belongs to such as these." —Luke 18:16*

The core lie is the central devaluing lie in our lives. It lodges in us at such an early age that we are unable to recognize it as the ultimate source of most, if not all of the issues of our lives. Our whole lives organize around it as the interpretive lens we see life through because it enters during our most vulnerable, formative years. I have only prayed with seven people who knew what their core lie was before Jesus revealed it to them in our sessions together. That stunning statistic shows just how deceptively the enemy manipulates lives, including those of born-again lovers of Jesus.

Emotions increase memory

Satan and his demonic interrogators have had the benefit of thousands of years to experiment with and study the intricate workings of the body, soul, and spirit of every human being. The evil seen during the Nazi-inspired Holocaust is a physical example of what has transpired for millennia in the spirit realm. Satan and his underlings have learned that the emotional part of our soul has infinitely more capacity for memory than our intellectual side. In physical anatomy, it's the difference between the right hemisphere of the brain and the left. It's the part of us that explains why we can hear two strokes of a guitar and are able to sing all the lyrics to a song from ten years earlier.

It also explains why, at a very early age, the enemy inspires an emotionally charged event to implant the core lie in our hearts like a button. Because emotions were involved during the implanting process, we remember the lie in our hearts until Jesus does heart surgery to remove it. Once the button is in place, the enemy uses people and circumstances to push it in order to program our hearts with a predictable response.

What your ancestors did, matters

Generational or bloodline sins, iniquities, and transgressions can undoubtedly be involved in the formation and implementation of core lies. These open doors to generations past not only make us vulnerable to the creation of core lies in our hearts but can grant the enemy access to block and attack our destinies, finances, bodies, and souls, leading to a range of problems. These generational issues can also include strongholds, curses, word curses, vows, oaths, sin patterns, mental issues, unexplainable deaths, and suicides. I have seen and heard of a variety of unexplainable manifestations that were resolved once bloodlines were cleansed through repentance and deliverance. The testimonies that follow after repenting on behalf of the bloodlines and cleansing them through the blood of Jesus are astounding.

What many excuse as genetic issues are nothing more than unrepentant sins, iniquities, and transgressions of ancestors. These open doors to the enemy become generations of strongholds and are tolerated as family traits or flaws. Left unrepented, these iniquities become the closet the enemy uses to lock away generations of destiny. Frequently, the padlocks on the doors of these destiny closets serve as the coping strategies people use to deal with the pain of believing core lies. We keep these hidden strongholds tucked away, just out of the reach of Jesus.

Jesus' blood cleanses our blood

We will continue to look at different aspects of generational issues that start here in Pattern 2 and continue to show up through the patterns as we move forward to Pattern 7. Bloodlines can be brought before the throne of God for cleansing at any point, as the Holy Spirit reveals the issues of generations past. Sometimes, they are revealed all at once, and sometimes, they are revealed a little at a time. Jesus paid the full price for us to represent our generations before the throne confidently and cleanse our bloodlines through His blood, which will open us up to the favor and blessings of the Father.

Guilt from generations past has a clear Biblical precedent.

"Who keeps lovingkindness for thousands, who forgives iniquity, transgression, and sin; yet He will by no means leave the guilty unpunished, visiting the iniquity of fathers on the children and on the grandchildren to the third and fourth generations."
—Exodus 34:7

If you are challenged by this statement's being an Old Covenant principal, I understand; I had the same issue when I was first exposed to it. I agree with you that every curse was broken, and every sin forgiven at the cross. But the cross has to be applied on an individual basis to receive its full effect. If you acquired a thousand acres through your bloodline and had the title deed in your hand, legally it is yours, no question. But you have squatters on your land that have been there for generations, and you want them gone. You have two choices. The first is to complain and say they have no legal right to be there. The second is to apply the deed and have them removed. The first will render the same results as generations past. The latter will remove the squatters, and you can experience the freedom to fully use every part of your land without hindrance. This demonstrates what the cleansing power of repenting for generational issues and then applying the cross and the blood of Jesus does to your bloodline. It also cleanses the curses that have come upon you through your ancestors.

The prophets did it

It was the protocol of the prophets of Israel as they would confess the sins, iniquities, and transgression of their forefathers. They did this to cleanse the pollution of the land that was preventing God's blessing and allowing enemy destruction and various other problems throughout Israel. Geographies and bloodlines have testimonies that demand us to present them before the Lord for Him to return them back in a cleansed and blessed state.

"He said, 'What have you done? The voice of your brother's blood is crying (testifying) to Me from the ground.'" — *Genesis 4:10 10*

It affected Joseph

Most of us will find ourselves in a combined state of blessing from the Lord, and at the same time, hindered by the enemy in certain areas. This was true of Joseph throughout his sojourn in Egypt. God's hand was on him, and he prospered wherever he went, yet generational issues were holding him back. From Potiphar's house to prison, to Pharaoh's house, Joseph prospered, no matter what the enemy threw at him. This was the fulfillment of the Abrahamic covenant of blessing to his generational lines. Abraham, Isaac, Jacob, and Joseph unquestionably had the financial favor and blessing of heaven over their lives. However, you can also see the stain of sins, iniquities, and transgressions showing up in their bloodline, and in Joseph's life, as well.

We can see the same Cain spirit that manifested between Jacob and Esau rear its jealous, hate-filled head between Joseph and his brothers. This spirit manifested as the primary agent the enemy, used to deliver the punch to Joseph's heart, destiny and gifting that he thought would take him out. And it almost did, except for the fact that God's hand was on him. The whole time the enemy was orchestrating Joseph's demise, God was plotting to ultimately beat the devil with his own stick.

Revelation changes perception

Quoting a passage thousands of times is no guarantee that you have the deeper revelation about its meaning. I have quoted the following passage thousands of times to explain inner healing and deliverance: *"For the weapons of our warfare are not of the flesh, but divinely powerful for the destruction of fortresses. We are destroying speculations, and every lofty thing raised up against the knowledge of God, and we are taking every thought captive to the obedience of Christ."* — *2 Corinthians 10:4-5*

Strongholds, lies about ourselves, and lies about God

As I was putting this passage into a training manual one day, the Holy Spirit spoke to my spirit, "Would you like to know what that passage means?" I started to laugh and responded with, "Yes, I thought I knew what it meant since I had quoted it thousands of times." He said, "There are three main ways the enemy attacks your freedom, and all three are found in that passage." They are strongholds, lies you believe about yourselves, and lies you believe about God. These three work together to form a web over your life to keep you trapped. The enemy can now assault you with tactics that will make you think that the tactics themselves are the reason for your captivity. His true strategy is actually in the material of the web.

Strategy and tactics

Every good battle plan has a strategic plan and a tactical plan. The enemy wants to keep you reacting to tactics so you cannot see his strategy. This passage reveals both. If you will respond to Jesus and destroy the strategic part of Satan's plan, you won't have to fight all of his tactics. They will be weakened and destroyed when you partner with heaven to thwart his strategic plan for your life.

Strongholds

He showed me that the first of the three are strongholds or fortresses depending on your translation. Analogous to enemy forts on friendly soil, strongholds are areas of the soul we have lost control of to the demonic realm. They can be anything from thoughts and behaviors to physical maladies we cannot seem to bring under the Lordship of Jesus and into alignment with who we really are in Him. We should be to bring them into submission to the Lordship of Jesus, but instead they control us.

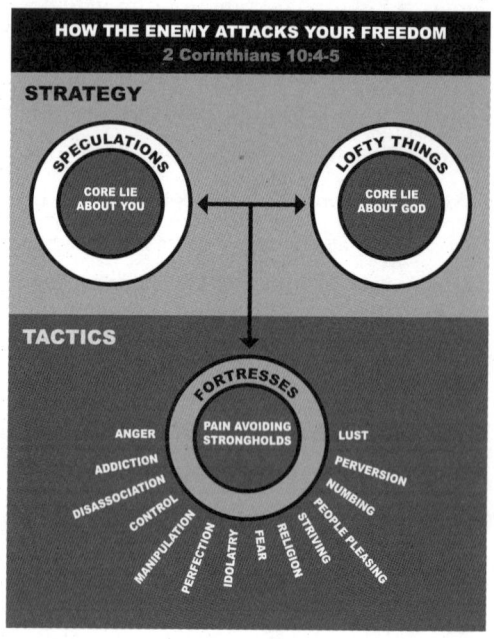

You can imagine what kind of damage a foreign enemy could do in America if they had a fortified military base in Washington DC. This analogy explains a stronghold or fortress in the realm of the soul, but there's great news. We have the powerful weapons of truth, deliverance, and divine encounter to destroy strongholds.

We discover the stronghold, break the agreement with the foundational lie of the stronghold through repentance, then command the spirits associated with it to go in Jesus' name. This destroys the stronghold. The brick and mortar of most strongholds are lies. Strongholds can also have a root of generational iniquity as well. To keep the stronghold from returning, we have to displace the lies that allow the construction of it, with the truth of Jesus, and relentlessly stay on guard against any agreement with that lie again. This is done by fixing our eyes on Jesus.

Speculations (lies about ourselves)

The Holy Spirit then showed me that the second way the enemy destroys our freedom is through the lies we believe about ourselves. This part of the passage says, "We are destroying speculations." Another translation says, "imaginations" instead of "speculations." This describes the core lie the enemy puts in our hearts at such an early age, as speculations or imaginations. We seldom recognize it as a lie; we only recognize the manifestation of it, which typically feels like insecurity. Many times, the early reinforcement of the core lie occurs through the family system we grow up in. The generational sins, iniquities, and transgressions that opened the door in the family line play a considerable role in enslaving everyone into the family system.

Core lies

The core lie programming strategy will be continually used as long as we cooperate with it. Left undetected, it seems to be the central focus of the three main components of the strategy the enemy uses to destroy the very freedom Jesus paid a high price for us to live in. The core lie is the spinal cord of all the other lies because the root of most of the issues of our lives can find their origins there. All splinter lies, coping strategies and demonic attachments branch off the core lie like nerves coming off of a spinal cord. When Jesus cuts the core lie spinal cord with His scalpel of truth, all the other issues will start to lose their strength.

Lofty things (lies about God)

The Holy Spirit showed me the third way the enemy destroys our freedom are lies we believe about God. That part of the passage reads, "And every lofty thing raised up against the knowledge of God." These core lies about God can be implanted in our hearts in a lot of different ways and sometimes enter through the same events as the core lies about us, but they can also come to us through corresponding family members, and just as many come to us, or get reinforced through defective theology. The theology you allow to enter your heart has a direct impact on your soul, and therefore, your life. Faulty theology can be espoused by anyone, no matter how many designatory letters a person has behind his or her name. The letters "Ph.D." are no guarantee that the person who wields those letters has embraced the true nature and character of God, no matter how many scriptures he or she uses to support his or her views.

We will never truly fall in love with God as long as we don't honestly know Him. Some theological conclusions about God create a confusing view of Him where He appears trustworthy one minute and unpredictable the next. It can cause our heart to view God in the same unpredictable way that many of us have experienced with our earthly fathers. He becomes the kind of Father who indiscriminately inflicts harm, and abandons us at the same time; He says He loves us and demands we love Him back. He becomes the Father who might even kick us out of the house if we don't keep the rules of the house to His satisfaction. At the same time, we will be required to trust Him and love Him with all our heart, soul, and mind.

Have you ever wondered why loving God felt so impossible? It's because deep in the core of your being, which was made in the image of God, you instinctively know you cannot love someone you don't trust. You were purposely created to be ridiculously in love with God, who is love, and who is truth, all at the same time. God cannot choose to love, because He is love. He cannot choose to tell the truth, because He is truth. Your very soul was manufactured as a reservoir to hold a pure deposit of Him.

Lies pollute

When you have perceptions of Him trying to fill that reservoir in you with something distorted, everything inside of your heart will react to the distortion no matter how desperately your head tries to adjust to it. Whether you know it or not, your heart is in a desperate search to find that pure drop of Him to hit your thirsty soul and make it come alive. Living water only comes from Him, and nothing else will make you come fully alive.

Core lies are the enemies' way of polluting that pure drop of God so that it never touches our soul, at least in its purest form. I gained clarity on this as I pressed into the new revelation of 2 Corinthians 10. The core lies we believe about God are lies we believe about the Father and Jesus. I have yet to discover a core lie about the Holy Spirit. There are many lies we believe about Him. Even though I have yet to run across someone with a core lie about the Holy Spirit, I know we will eventually see those core lies surface about Him.

Core lies about the Father and Jesus work in concert with the core lie we believe about ourselves to create a network of lies and strongholds over our destiny, and gifting the way a spider suffocates its prey in a tangled web. Many times, we can't even see that we are caught because we have been in the web so long that it feels comfortably uncomfortable. We don't recognize how much bondage we have been tolerating until Jesus wields His sword to cut us out of it. I have seen people's countenance, and posture completely change over a two-hour session. In fact, I have seen several physical conditions healed right in front of me as people are rescued by Jesus from the spider web they have been calling their lives.

Physical healing through inner healing

An example of this is a lady I prayed with, and I wished I had captured a before-and-after picture to document my time with her. She came into the room hunched over, barely able to walk, entirely oppressed, and in severe pain. We had to lean in just to hear her weak, quiet voice because she was so shut down by the enemy. Her very presence leaked sadness, depression, oppression, and pain into the room. She had a condition called complex regional pain syndrome (CRPS) and lived in a toxic environment with dysfunctional, demonized family members where she was the primary caregiver.

CRPS causes lasting pain in legs and arms and can manifest after an injury. She had been in a car wreck that seemed to be the catalyst for this part of her condition. As I led her through prayer and Jesus started cutting the web of lies and demonic spirits off of her, she began to sit up in the chair straight and started to smile a little more with every expulsion of one of her demons. At the end of the session, with the lies exposed and truth reclaimed and the afflicting spirits expelled, I commanded healing in every part of her body in Jesus' name.

Every bit of pain left her body along with all the stiffness, to the point that she was able to walk around the room without a limp for the first time in years. She then started kneeling all the way to the ground and back up to test the healing. She previously could not even bend her knees. Frequently, physical healing happens once demons are made to vacate our bodies and the lies they are attached to get replaced with the truth of Jesus. This shouldn't surprise us since scripture is full of examples of Jesus casting spirits out of people, with physical healing happening as a result.

It's about strategy, not tactics

Her story reveals how the enemy can use multiple, ground level, battle tactics against us in so many numerous and varied ways that we forget the path back to their ultimate strategic source. All of the tactical ways with which he executes his battle plan can usually be traced back to the strategic part of his plan of implanting lies we believe about us, and lies we believe about God in order to create stronghold responses to the lies. Seeing the attacks of the enemy through these over-arching strategies that cause us to respond to the stronghold tactics will simplify the war we in which we are engaged. This understanding will keep us from getting blinded by the numerous tactics he uses against us. An understanding of how the enemy attempts to destroy our freedom and disconnect us from the prophetic words of the womb and from God will come to us not only on a tactical level but also on a strategic level.

Core lies are his core attack

I cannot overemphasize the need to understand these three core lies and how they have impacted every area of our lives. In fact, the strongholds mentioned in that same passage, many times are nothing more than how we cope with the devaluing results of believing those three lies reinforced by demonic attachments. Regular encounters with Jesus and His truths will allow Him to sever the core lies and cause the need to cope to go away. In fact, every bit of bondage the lady was in with CRPS could be traced right back to her core lies and how they had perverted her view of herself and God. This perversion caused her to tolerate the spiderweb she was caught in for years. Throw in a little bad theology along with her devalued heart, and she even believed she deserved the debilitating pain as well as the devaluing comments from family members that came with regularity.

It's not complicated

The enemy wants you to think that obtaining freedom is such a complicated mess to wade through that you will never get your healing and freedom. Jesus keeps it simple, and understanding this spiritual journey becomes very attainable through Him. One thing is for sure; You can't fix yourself or even accurately diagnose the patterns without Him. You might mentally comprehend the patterns, but He has to give you the answers and the power to destroy the strongholds, speculations, and lofty things. A little bit of truthful information applied in the flesh is more dangerous than complete ignorance. It can keep you chasing the loop of a wrong answer in your head for years, thinking one more loop around and you will finally chase down the right solution that will let you figure it all out.

Jesus is the only healer

I have had the privilege of partnering with Jesus as two different ladies, who were the victims of childhood sexual abuse, got set free from a lifetime of bondage in two hours with Jesus. Both of them had been in therapy for over 40 years. One was in bondage to a lie about God's approval of her abuse, and the other was set free from an abusive memory that she had blocked for almost 60 years. I am not trying to be critical of counseling or therapy, but I am critical of counseling or therapy that doesn't champion Jesus as the only one who heals. True healing that lasts doesn't come from knowledge or a technique; it comes from an encounter with Jesus.

The enemy knows solutions to find healing apart from Jesus don't exist. He wants us living lives separated from Jesus, our gifting, and destiny before we ever get a chance to discover them. I get to watch God on a daily basis re-connect people to their gifting, destiny, and call through encounters with Him. Many times when the connection occurs, it brings the recipient to tears because their destiny has been in their heart from the womb, and they feel it when the reconnection happens. Healing always brings reconnection with heavens' intentions for our lives.

Gifting is always attacked

Seers are great examples of the enemy attacking gifting. I have encountered shut-down seers so many times that I have lost count. In the Old Testament, a seer was another term for prophets but has been adopted in some Christian circles as a term for gifted individuals who can see into the spiritual realm. They see angels, demons, and pictures of things that are going on in the spiritual environment they are in at the time.

The enemy hates seers

The first time it happened, I was praying with Jim. I was about 30 minutes into our session, and he was pretty blocked. He wasn't hearing God's voice and wasn't really seeing any visions either. I then listened to the Holy Spirit say to me that Jim was a "seer," and I knew what He was telling me to do. I asked Jim if he saw demons when he was very young and he said, oh, yes. "They used to scare the heck out me!" I asked if he used to have night terrors, as well, and he said, "Yes, they were awful." I then asked him if he saw visions now, and he said no. Next, I asked him if he had dreams, and he said no.

I led him through a prayer to break the vow that he made not to see, hear or feel in the spirit realm. As soon as he broke the vow, he described what happened next as someone flipping on a light switch. He started immediately having visions, with his eyes open, and hearing the voice of God through thoughts, and feeling His presence. Jim went on to be used by the ministry with which he was involved to give detailed insight into what was going on in the regions and churches they did ministry in. He started functioning in gifts that had not been previously accessible to him. He was now able to walk in a new part of the destiny God had spoken to him in the womb but that he was completely unaware of before our prayer.

Rooms, doors, rats, and garbage

By using an analogy of your soul to a house, you can quickly understand how the enemy divides your heart and prevents you from moving forward in your destiny and purpose with a singleness of heart. When you received Jesus, you opened up the front door of your house and let Him in, but there are cabinets, closets, and rooms in your house that you don't even know are there, let alone the key to unlocking them. Locked away behind those doors there is typically garbage and rats feeding on the trash. The garbage represents the wounds, lies, pain, and pain-avoiding strongholds inspired by the enemy. The rats represent the demons that attend the doors to those cabinets, closets, and rooms. They are attached to, and feeding on the garbage.

The inner healing component to your freedom journey amounts to giving Jesus access to any door of your house that He is knocking on, to heal the pain and trauma of the wounds and expose the lies we are believing *(Rev. 3:20)*. In essence, He removes the doors and takes the garbage out of the house. The deliverance part includes breaking agreements with the lies behind the doors, which cuts off the access the demonic has to the rooms. We then exercise the authority Jesus has given us to command them to go in Jesus' name. That room will no longer have a door, and the garbage and rats are gone. Jesus just integrated another part of your heart into Him. Being one spirit with Him becomes more of a reality every time we open one of these doors and let Jesus in.

You have to do both

I have seen way too much to agree with those who believe that all your issues result from demonic infestation. Many in deliverance seem to believe that all of your issues are the rats that are in the house. This implies that if you kick the rats out of the house, you don't really have to deal with the garbage. If you get the rats out but leave the garbage in the house, how long will it be before the rats come back? I have also seen way too much to agree with those who believe that all you have to do is take out the garbage through inner healing and you don't have to deal with the rats (demons). If you take the garbage out but leave the rats in the house, they will find something else to destroy.

I am very deliberate about both inner healing and deliverance and have thousands of success stories to prove that this approach is not only biblical but effective. Jesus came to heal the brokenhearted, and He commanded us to cast out demons. He did both and equipped us with both because we need to do both.

Powerful weapons

We have divinely powerful weapons available to us, according to *2 Corinthians 10:4-5*. These weapons deal with deliverance (destroying strongholds). They also deal with core lies about us (destroying speculations), and core lies about God (and every lofty thing raised up against the knowledge of God). The reason we have divinely powerful weapons that deal with both inner healing and deliverance is because we need them. God will never give us spiritual tools that we don't need.

They are effective

I witness the effectiveness of these weapons every time Jesus revisits a memory when the core lie entered the heart of a person for the first time. This strategic unveiling of the schemes of the enemy exposes the devaluing memories of the enemy to the healing touch of Jesus. He releases all the emotional pain locked behind those doors of guarded memories and speaks truth into the lies, where most of the pain is stored. Lie-based pain accurately describes what most people are trying to keep locked up in closets in their hearts. Lies contain most of the pain in a memory.

Lie-based pain

The enemy wants us to think that what happened to us causes all the pain in a memory because it seems harder to fix. The lie you started believing about yourself and God as a result of the event is where most of the pain in a memory is coming from, not the experience itself. The lie is the thorn stuck in the body that is causing all the infectious pain to spread like poison to the whole person. How the thorn got injected into the body becomes almost irrelevant once the thorn is removed.

Heart programming

Based on my experience, I believe Joseph's core lie had already entered his heart at seven years old or younger. But by the time he has his first dream in the Biblical timeline, he was 17. By this age, we already see the effects, through Joseph's response, to years of programming from his core lie within his family system. That system had programmed his heart through brotherly rejection and parents trying to manage a very gifted boy in the plain site of jealous brothers. Any system that works to suppress the exceptional, to prevent feelings of inferiority in others, creates even more significant issues because God does not sponsor those actions. God will never place the extremely gifted in our midst so that we can suppress them. That activity devalues the talented and sends a clear demonic message to everyone else. If people stand out in life and walk in their God-given destiny, we should not criticize them.

The brothers still recognized the special treatment of Joseph even though it was negative, and it didn't decrease their jealousy one bit. Even though Joseph was Jacob's favorite, it seemed that he tried to minimize the perception of his favoritism by criticizing the God-given dreams of Joseph. The enemy can use any circumstance as soil to plant a core lie in, but this was fertile ground for the seed to grow in until it was time to transplant it into the fertile soil of the Nile River Delta of Egypt.

The way that Joseph rubbed the prophetic dreams in his brothers' and parents' faces seems to express his coping response to years of rejection and suppression. His response was created by years of the enemy triggering the core lie in Joseph's soul through his family system. Based on the evidence in the story, I am willing to speculate that Joseph's core lie was; "I don't matter." Before you dismiss this as a possibility, realize that core lies contradict the reality of what God has for someone. It seems to me, the exact opposite of a world leader would be someone who doesn't matter, even a slave. And that is what Joseph precisely became for 13 years in Egypt. His brothers, through this act, revealed a pattern of bullying and devaluing of Joseph that had been firmly established long before they sold him into slavery.

That could explain why Joseph seemed to flaunt his dreams to his brothers and father, in anticipation of their rejection, which had the apparent meaning of them bowing down before him. It also reveals a history of using his gifts to cope with the pain of his core lie which will also appear in Pattern 4. There certainly wasn't a lot of humility or wisdom utilized when Joseph shared his dreams.

Core lies create value deficits

Core lies are designed to create value deficits in the hearts of its victims. Deficits are designed to get us chasing after value from the things of this Earth. The cravings we develop for these value idols are in direct proportion to the level of devaluation and deception our hearts have undergone. The devaluation of the heart deepens with each idol's failure to bring value back into the heart of its victim. Idols are designed that way. They are under the same law of diminishing returns as anything else we seek for value apart from Jesus. It's why addiction is on an ever-diminishing treadmill that requires more and more to accomplish the same pain-numbing effect.

You have to get value from somewhere. In fact, you were designed to have eternal value and be valuable. It's as if you were born with a cord and a plug to receive value. Whatever you plug into owns you. Plug into Jesus, and you get set free from the cravings of obtaining value from the things and people of this Earth. Plug into anything else, and you become a slave to whatever you plug into. The more the heart gets devalued from the core lie, the deeper the craving and search for value become. Addictions are born out of the womb of a devalued heart.

Core lies blind our hearts to our real value and identity and persuade us to settle for the crumbs the enemy doles out to devalue us even more. Someone with a core lie of "I'm unworthy" will be susceptible to relationships with people who will use, abuse, and devalue them further. Believing they are unworthy of real love, they are willing to settle for whatever they can get, and what they get is whatever the enemy serves up on a big plate of dysfunction. Lust becomes the cheap intimacy substitute for the devalued heart. The illusions of connection and security get paid for at the high price of further devaluation and slavery.

Lies repel gifting

Most of the time our core lies are in direct opposition to our gifting, destiny, and call. My sister-in-law Cherry and I were praying with a lady one day, and Cherry got a prophetic word that this lady was an evangelist. I immediately got the same word confirming it. The lady broke down crying and said, "This word resonates deep in my heart, but how can that be? Ever since the day that I received Jesus at age seven, I have doubted my salvation." Her core lie of "I'm not good enough" was crafted just for her so that she would not be able to step into her destiny and evangelize the lost. The enemy had exiled her to the island of "I'm not good enough" and therefore had shut her down from sharing a gospel that she couldn't seem to believe for herself. She felt not good enough to be saved and certainly not good enough to share the gospel and live out the words of the womb for her life.

It doesn't have to be bad

The events in which core lies get planted aren't always a devastating or even harmful event. Sometimes the event seems insignificant when the seed gets planted. The lie may not get fully activated until a more opportune time. I received, through a word of knowledge, the age that the core lie entered for this young man I was praying with. When he asked Jesus to show him the memory, he saw himself at age five falling off his bike and his dad lovingly helping him get back up on his bike and encouraging him to keep going. The core lie got planted that day that he was not enough.

God showed him it wasn't about the fall, but from that point forward he had compared himself to his dad and had always come up short and never felt like he was enough. His dad was a very loving father and amazing pastor that everyone loved. This young man was also called to be a pastor but could never seem to fully step into his gifting because he never felt like he was enough compared to his dad. Destiny handcuffs were placed on him at age five, but he didn't even know they were there until he slowly tried to step into his destiny over time. When he met with me, he knew that something was holding him back but had no idea what it was.

Lies get planted early

Core lies, like seeds, get planted in the heart early and fertilized and watered along the way by people and circumstances. The purpose is to co-mingle and pervert the great harvest of truth in the heart planted by the prophetic words of God in the womb. This can be applied to the parable of the wheat and tares taught by Jesus in Matthew 13 verses 36 through 44. Even though this is obviously an end-times passage, aspects of the concept seem to fit individuals and the choices we make over a lifetime. The enemy sows weeds (core lies) at night (we don't see it happening) in the field that has been planted by the master (the prophetic words of the womb).

The Master's plan

The Master doesn't pull up the weeds until the harvest so that the difference between the weeds and the grain is apparent. Core lies are usually not recognizable until they bear fruit. We seldom realize we have issues until the seeds of pain grow into the weeds of pain-avoiding strongholds. When we surrender, God starts to gather and burn the weeds in the field of our hearts so the yield of the grain of our lives will bring in a clean and abundant harvest.

Who God is to us in Pattern 2: **Yahweh Shammah = The Lord is There**
Yahweh Shammah is the name declared for Jerusalem in the book of
Ezekiel in chapter 48 verse 35. It's the name of God that indicates
His very nature will not allow Him to leave you in ruins. He always
brings restoration, it's part of His identity to do so. It's the part of His
heart that we cling to, which brings healing to the wounds, destroys
the core lies of the enemy and cleanses bloodlines. It's the vision of
Jesus that proves He was there in the core lie memories. The Lord is
there to shatter the lens the enemy formed over our eyes through an
early onslaught against ours identities and the Lord's true identity.
That Lord destroys the pain from that early preemptive strike which
comes from the lie that God wasn't there. His very name declares that
He is the God that is always there. As our hearts attune to this part of
His, we will cry out like David in *Psalm 139; "Where can I go from Your
Spirit? Or where can I flee from Your presence?"* It's the part of God's heart
that testifies to us from heaven through the blood of Jesus, "I will not
leave you in a ruinous state, I will restore and bind up your broken
heart." The Lord who is there always has a truthful, healing response
to the speculations about you and the lofty things the enemy raises up
against the true identity of God. He truly is the Lord who is there.

*Scripture: "For the weapons of our warfare are not of the flesh, but divinely
powerful for the destruction of fortresses. We are destroying speculations, and
every lofty thing raised up against the knowledge of God, and we are taking every
thought captive to the obedience of Christ," —2 Corinthians 10:4-5*

Tool: Memory/core lie

Activation:
- Ask Jesus to reveal the core lie that you believe about yourself.
- Once the lie is revealed, ask Him to show you the memory it came
  in through.
- Ask Jesus to show you where He was in the memory.
- Ask Him to show you what He is doing with that lie and the truth

He is replacing it with.

- Ask that all of it be nailed to the cross and cleansed with the blood of Jesus all the way back to Adam and forward.
- Cut all unholy soul and spiritual ties with your generational lines and all sex partners outside of marriage, including any images of pornography.
- Ask Jesus what spirits are present.
- Command every spirit He names associated with the core lie to leave in Jesus' name.
- Continue to command until you sense that every spiritual attachment has left.
- Ask for the Holy Spirit to fill you back up and to release you into your full destiny in Him.

JOSEPH PRAYER

Pattern 3:

Repetition fertilizes lies

The enemy reinforces lies through people and circumstances

Joseph's Pattern 3: The weeds of wounds and lies, now sprouting in the heart of Joseph were fertilized through the false allegations of Potiphar's wife. Prison was the perfect greenhouse for the enemy to grow reaction in Joseph's heart through the devaluation of doing prison time for a rape he didn't commit. It was an attempt to get Joseph to instinctively react to life through the distorted lens of his core lie programmed through devaluing interactions with people and circumstances. It seems the enemy could have been setting up soul triggers for him to expect rejection to follow every promotion. His father gave him a coat of many colors, and his brothers rejected him. God gave him dreams and not only did his brothers reject him but so did his parents. What's less than a slave? It is a criminal, who's in prison. But the anointing of leadership and the favor of God was so apparent on Joseph that he rose to the top no matter where the enemy placed him, whether in Potiphar's house, prison or with Pharaoh.

"Now when his master heard the words of his wife, which she spoke to him, saying, 'This is what your slave did to me,' his anger burned. So Joseph's master

took him and put him into the jail, the place where the king's prisoners were confined; and he was there in the jail." — *Genesis 39:19-20*

Joseph's repetitive pain pattern: He experiences more rejection, and false accusations, and now imprisonment. The enemy wanted him to move out of expectant destiny to expectant pain and rejection, and out of faith and into unbelief.

Joseph's probable lies from the enemy: You're not a leader, you can't even determine what you eat or when you go to bed. God is punishing you with prison for the lust you had in your heart for Potiphar's wife. God is not going to follow through for you because you don't matter.

One strategic punch, landed in the right spot, at the right time sets a lifetime of devaluation in motion. Like an expert fighter, the enemy creates a tender spot in the heart through the core lie and then exploits it through repeated punches to that same spot. These constant attacks are fertilizer on the lie that was planted in the hole in the heart, dug with the sharp scalpel of pain. These precise, repetitive attacks program the ways that a person will respond to circumstances and people. Sometimes, the enemy will let the core lie lay dormant until the appropriate time to take the pain of this lie to a deeper level. The enemy's goal is that we come into agreement with his lies by driving them so deeply into our hearts that we don't even recognize our cooperation with our own suffering.

Low life

With every devaluing punch, our agreement with the core lie gets reinforced. As the enemy pokes the same sore spot of the heart so that we learn not to expect too much out of life, people, ourselves, and even God. Retreat becomes a safer place to live unless we swing to the opposite reaction and try to make life and everyone we encounter bow to our will to succeed. Either activity achieves the goal of the enemy because both options are living in reaction to the enemy instead of in response to Jesus.

We are trained in our heart to respond to life the way the demonic programmers desire. The programming intensifies with every devaluing event, trying to force us to come into agreement with a false identity. That identity will be diametrically opposed to the one prophesied over us in the womb. Without understanding what is happening, we come under the reign and rule of the lie rather than the reign and rule of King Jesus. We blame it on genetics, abuse, karma, a sinful nature, or circumstances without ever attributing it to the real source of the programming of our hearts, which is the demonic realm.

Fight the real enemy

Paul tells us, in the book of Ephesians, chapter 6 verse 12, that we are not struggling with flesh and blood but various ranks of demons that have been assigned to thwart God's plans:

"For our struggle is not against flesh and blood, but against the rulers, against the powers, against the world forces of this darkness, against the spiritual forces of wickedness in the heavenly places."—Ephesians 6:12

You aren't at war with you

Have you ever read that passage with the understanding that the flesh and blood with which you are not struggling with, includes your own? This passage makes a blanket statement about all flesh and blood not being our struggle, yet most of us assume the passage only refers to not struggling with the flesh and blood of other people. We are flesh and blood, and therefore not struggling with flesh and blood has to apply to us as well. If that is true, then the implication means you are not really struggling with yourself either. Real freedom will break out in your heart if you understand that you are not in a fight with yourself. This releases a truth that we all need to catch; God is not asking you to struggle to control your flesh. He is asking you to surrender your flesh to the Holy Spirit, not to wrestle with it.

You have to be awakened to the reality that you are in a spiritual struggle with demons assaulting your heart and destiny from the day of your birth. They are just using a flesh and blood smoke screen of people and circumstances to hide what they are up to. We spend a large portion of our lives not recognizing that demons are training our hearts with constant pain, trauma, and pleasure to create a conditioned response. Without our conscious knowledge of it, our heart is being trained to respond to pain and pleasure the way experts train service dogs to respond to threats. Triggers of the soul are conditioned responses to pain and pleasure that have been inflicted over a period of time. They continue working until the reaction becomes a predictable yet uncontrollable reflex of the soul called a "stronghold" in Scripture.

Pain seeks pleasure

Since pain seeks pleasure, the enemy will hit us with pain and, alternately, hand us the means to self-medicate. Once programmed, all the enemy has to do is push 'play' on the core lie button, through people and circumstances, for the conditioned response desired at that moment. The reactions to the painful stimuli become as predictable to the enemy as telling a trained service dog to attack after it has been through a repetitive training pattern a thousand times. The enemy can now use our strongholds to program other friends and family into an interconnected system of core lies and pain-avoiding strongholds. These systems are designed to create the greatest adverse effect on the group and the individuals within the group. The result sought after is the one most likely to limit or shut down each person's chance to live out their God-given gifting and destiny.

Once the enemy has programmed our hearts to his music, we dance like the organ grinder's monkey every time he turns the crank and plays the music. This dance of our false self is in direct contradiction to that of the original self that God created us to have and the destiny He has planned for us. That monkey, like our heart, gets trained in multiple ways. It first starts out with pain. The organ grinder inflicts pain on the monkey to get it to dance. Once it starts to dance, he then rewards it with a pleasurable treat. As the monkey begins to respond enthusiastically to the music to get the treat, the organ grinder gives the treat but also responds with a higher reward of affection and value. The organ grinder receives the applause of the people, and the system of programming gets locked into an ever-growing cyclical pattern.

Respond; don't react

If we fall for the trap of people and circumstances as the central issue of our lives, then we will become slaves to the people and circumstances we encounter on a daily basis. Our life becomes an unsolvable journey if we believe this to be true. We become trapped, vacillating somewhere between anger, fear, control, despair, and self-medication. This mindset sets us up for a lifetime of reactions because you cannot control someone else's flesh with your flesh. You cannot even control your own flesh with your flesh. Only our spirit, led by the Holy Spirit, can bring our flesh into alignment with holy living *(Gal. 5:16)*. This deep connection will prevent us from seeking solutions to holy living apart from the Holy Spirit and will free us from the bondage of trying to become the sin managers of ourselves and others.

Jesus dependent

We ignore the real spiritual issues and attachment to circumstantial patterns at our own peril. We also ignore the reality of Romans 6 and what that reality will produce in our lives if we come into agreement with it. We will go into greater detail of being set free from sin in Pattern 6. Let's just say for now that Jesus has emancipated you from sin and its power, source, and effect. This completely eliminates the need for us to become enslaved to a spirit of control. We will be set free to become Jesus-dependent and not people- and circumstance-dependent. This will set us free from control, the most common quicksand in the human condition.

You have authority

Jesus declared in Matthew 28, after His resurrection, that He had all authority in heaven and on earth. It's by that authority that He commissions His followers to act on His behalf to expand His Kingdom from heaven to earth. If Jesus has all authority, that means that by default, the only authority the enemy has access to is the authority we give him. We do this by coming into agreement with his lies.

Don't eat the fruit

It's a daily replay of the Garden of Eden; choose to see our lives through the lens of the Father, or look through the enemy's distorted lens of determining good and evil for ourselves. Every time we make a decision independently of the Holy Spirit, we take another bite of that death producing fruit from the Garden of Eden. The only tree that was guarded when our ancient ancestors were expelled from the Garden was the tree of life, and that was because God did not want us living forever in a sin-saturated, disease-ridden, condition. The tree of the knowledge of good and evil still produces a lot of fruit today. Such is the case even in Christian circles. Death-producing strongholds result in anyone who eats this fruit by determining good and evil for themselves apart from God.

Circumstances are the result of many things coming together all at a moment in time. Any given day is a combination of our choices, responses, the enemy's attacks and programming, generational sins, iniquities and transgressions, and God's attempts to get us on the path of destiny and blessing. It takes spiritual skill to learn what comes from the enemy, what comes from us, and what comes from the Lord.

Fix our eyes, open our ears

Listening to the Holy Spirit is the only way to stay in balance. We have to pay close enough attention to what circumstances might be telling us without being in bondage to them. We have to learn what we can from circumstances and at the same time fix our eyes on Jesus so that we respond and not react.

A fine line exists between ignoring circumstances and learning what you can from them. Circumstances can reveal issues that need to be dealt with in our own lives or in our generational lines. To just plow ahead in what we think is faith, while ignoring signs that something is blocking our destiny, will cause us to log decades striving in a barren wilderness while looking for God's plan, direction, and favor to no avail. This is the part of the wilderness where we can get trapped in the pit of blaming God and becoming angry with Him while rationalizing and turning to our self-medication of choice. We can burn decades in that wilderness if we don't recognize we have ventured off the ancient path. Nothing will shift until we change our mind and direction and get back on it.

"Thus says the Lord, 'Stand by the ways and see and ask for the ancient paths, Where the good way is, and walk in it; And you will find rest for your souls."
—Jeremiah 6:16

We cannot let circumstances define us but must also realize that the natural realm represents a life-sized mirror of our heart's posture in the spiritual realm. A surrendered heart, listening to the Holy Spirit, will be the only way to navigate our very nonlinear path in the spiritual realm. This uncertainty of hearing God's voice is why many reject living life this way. It's certainly not black and white and choosing to live by Biblical principal as opposed to hearing His voice comforts the mind but deadens the heart.

Listen up

Living by Biblical principals undoubtedly results in a better outcome than not doing so, but living from Biblical principals alone will never allow you to tap into God's best for you. Operating out of principal alone will cause you to run the risk of never discovering your true gifting, destiny, and call. That can only be found by getting close enough to Him to hear His whispers in your ear. He speaks by putting a thought in your mind that you didn't put there, and He never contradicts His written word. If your life is hidden in Jesus, as the Bible says, it requires you to get close enough to Him to hear His voice and find it.

None of this ignores the fact that the enemy most certainly attacks through people and circumstances. Peter tells us:
"Be on alert our enemy prowls around like a roaring lion looking for someone to devour." —1 Pet. 5:8

Deliverance brings healing

I had been out of town on a ministry trip, and when I got home, I found my wife very sick with a urinary tract infection. She was so ill that she ended up in the ER that night and was sent home with antibiotics and painkillers. Two days later things were worse, and we ended up back in the ER. Of course, I was praying for healing every step of the way, but to no avail. Next, the doctors were saying it was diverticulitis, and with more pain meds and more antibiotics, we were back at home. A day later, we were back in the ER, and now they said she might have appendicitis. I now knew for sure this was not just a physical issue but a spiritual one.

This just smelled like the enemy to me, and I started warring against them every way that I knew how. We were admitted to the hospital, and a day went by with the doctors watching her condition. I was trying to find the access or agreements the enemy had used to attack in this way, and I was just not getting any answers. The next morning she was scheduled for a CT scan, and I went deep into prayer, still looking for solutions that had not come yet. Up until that point, my wife had been on IV fluids because one small sip of any liquid had sent her doubled over in pain in her abdomen. I woke up that morning at about 4:00 am and went into tongues, out loud, in the room for about 30 minutes.

Bad energy

In the midst of my groaning, I heard the Holy Spirit speak to my spirit the word "massage," and I had the key to the attack that I had been looking for. My wife went through hip surgery a few months earlier, and her pudendal nerve was restricted by scar tissue. She was receiving physical therapy through massage each week to loosen the nerve entrapment. That week, her regular therapist had not been available, so someone else had done the treatment, and that was when all of the physical issues had started.

I had studied therapies based on the use of spiritual energy for healing, and since most practitioners rely on universal energy to flow through them, I had the answer I was looking for. I had my wife break agreement with the massage she had received from the last therapist, and I commanded that spirit to leave, and it lifted off of her body together with all the pain. I then commanded healing in Jesus name. I had just finished my prayer when the technician came in the room to give her two large cups of contrast die to drink for the CT scan.

The man of great faith that I am then said, "She can't drink all of that." One sip of anything had been causing her to double over in pain. My wife looked at me and said, "Let me try." She downed both cups with no problem. The CT scan came back clear, and we left the hospital after they watched her for a few more hours with no more pain and no more issues.

Sometimes it is tactics

That was a cheap attack by the enemy to damage and disrupt, and it had nothing to do with her core lie. It was a subtle agreement to a massage that she was unaware had a demonic source behind it. We have to stay on the alert and let the Holy Spirit reveal what we are up against each day in the war of the ages.

Ritual abuse

One of the cheapest shots I encounter of the enemy's programming of the heart that takes an even more sinister turn involves ritual abuse. It takes the programming concept and does it over a shorter, more intensely abusive period of time. Ritual abuse and Satanic ritual abuse are the two variations of this absolute evil perpetrated on children. I have encountered Satanic ritual abuse (SRA) multiple times and have had success reintegrating the hearts of some of the SRA victims.

Fractured, not forgotten

God, in His grace, looked down the corridors of time in human history and saw all the evil that was going to be perpetrated on children. He mercifully designed the human soul with the ability to fracture in order to spread the pain out over multiple personalities instead of just one. This allows the person to survive without the one personality imploding into insanity as a result of the pain and trauma inflicted through the abuse.

Dissociative identity disorder (DID), is the condition of having multiple personalities. Jesus also comes to reintegrate the personalities after they survive the abuse and grow out of childhood. Jesus says in Isaiah 61 that He came to bind up the brokenhearted. The Hebrew word *shabar* (which means fractured), is the word translated into *brokenhearted*. A fractured heart is precisely what happens during abuse, and I have watched the love of Jesus bind the separate pieces back together like a cast. This results with the personalities wholly integrated back together. SRA is a very specific issue with very specialized solutions and people who are called to that ministry. If you suspect you are SRA, seek out someone who has experience in this area, as typical deliverance and inner healing will not resolve your issues.

Jesus binds up the broken hearted

I was praying with a lady with DID, and as soon as she walked into the room, she said she had never felt present in her body. As we worked through our session together and interacted with her parts, a stunned look came over her face as she said to me, "I just saw all of my parts snap together. Is that normal?" I said, "Oh yeah, that's a good thing." She then said, "Is it possible that Jesus is re-wiring my brain?" I said, "Absolutely," and I got up and laid hands on her head, and she physically felt Him rewiring her brain as I prayed. She then said, "Oh my God! I feel the carpet under my feet." She then started describing the room in detail that we were in and said, "I am present in my body for the first time in my life." She started to weep, and so did I.

Open doors that need closing

Generational issues will continue to surface and usually more frequently at this stage if they haven't already. Family systems of intentional and unintentional programming can get entrenched and start conditioning our responses for the rest of our lives. Dealing with generational sins, iniquities, and transgressions is a necessary component of any freedom strategy.

Jesus has made the way for a generational blessing to flow from heaven through the devastating defeat He handed the enemy at the cross. Even under the Old Covenant, God described His nature to Moses on the mountain in this way:

"The Lord, the Lord God, compassionate and gracious, slow to anger, and abounding in lovingkindness and truth; who keeps lovingkindness for thousands, who forgives iniquity, transgression, and sin." —Exodus 34:6-7

Doors that need opening

Generational lovingkindness flows out from the blood of Jesus, but just like the blood of the lamb had to be applied to the doorposts of the Exodus generation's houses, the blood of Jesus has to be applied to the sins, iniquities, and transgressions of the bloodline to be effective.

The death angel did not pass over the houses that lacked the blood of the lamb on the doorpost during the Exodus from Egypt. The effects of iniquity in the bloodline don't automatically go away the day you receive Jesus even though the iniquity and its effects have been defeated. Most of the time there has to be intentional repenting and cleansing for that to occur. This is a principal and not a law since I have seen exceptions to this rule.

Gideon closed bloodline doors

The story of Gideon is a case study for cleansing the bloodline and the result of abundant life flowing from the cleansing. Gideon hides from his demonic oppressors, personified by the Amalekites who have so tormented and raided the Jews on a regular basis, that they have forced them to live in caves in the sides of mountains. These caves are described as strongholds. These are the circumstances that surround Jesus' appearance to Gideon in the wine press as he gathers wheat so his enemies won't steal from him. He's hiding from his enemies and he finds his destiny through the angel of the Lord.

Most occurrences of the angel of the Lord in the Old Testament are pre-incarnate visitations of Jesus. This seems to be the case as Jesus immediately speaks identity into a weak and fearful Gideon. Gideon blames his bloodline for being weak, but Jesus calls him a mighty warrior and proclaims that Gideon will defeat Israel's enemies as one man. This is Jesus revealing what was prophesied over Gideon in the womb and calling his heart back into a destiny that could not have been further from the reality Gideon was living. It is never Jesus' intent for us to hunker down in pits that our enemies provide to waste our lives there. The enemy hits Gideon right in his destiny and gifting. Gideon falls for it and is living like a coward instead of living according to the mighty warrior identity that was prophesied over him in the womb. I watch this same phenomenon on a daily basis. Abundant life is waiting for us, but it is outside the pit.

Idols fall

One of the requirements the Lord places on Gideon as he progresses from wimp to warrior is to tear down the idols of his father. In other words, He tells Gideon the same thing He tells you and me; if you are going to step into your destiny fully, you will have to deal with generational sins, iniquities, and transgressions of your bloodline. Gideon is going nowhere until he pulls those altars down off that hill and out of his own heart. The altars of Baal and the Asherah poles of generations past fall easily once Gideon sees himself through the eyes of the pre-incarnate Jesus. He starts to believe the words of the womb Jesus spoke to him in the wine press that destiny changing day. *"The Lord is with you, O valiant warrior... Surely I will be with you, and you shall defeat Midian as one man."* —*Judges 6:12b, 16*

Jesus helps him

God tells Gideon to utilize two bulls from his father, each seven years old in dealing with the demonic altars. The first bull tears them down, and the second bull is the sacrifice for the iniquities of his father. Jesus is symbolized by both bulls in Gideon's story. He is the strong bull from the Father that tears down the idolatrous strongholds in our hearts from our bloodlines. He is also the bull sacrificed for the iniquities associated with the idols and altars of past generations. Both are seven years old, picturing the perfection of Jesus and the completeness of the destruction of the strongholds in our hearts.

Unbelief is not the issue

Too frequently our circumstances reflect the idolatry of our generational lines combined with the unbelief the enemy has programmed into our heart. I am not a big fan of using the word unbelief to describe a person's lack of trusting God in any given area. The word unbelief implies there is a moment in our hearts when we do not believe something. That doesn't fit the reality that I face on a daily basis in prayer ministry. I don't see that we are ever without belief. The issue is not unbelief but *what* we believe. When I do not believe the truth, by default I believe lies. My heart is in a constant state of belief. Faith is the magnet that attracts whatever you believe into your life. If I start to think the circumstances of my life are an accurate portrayal of who I am, I will express faith in lies that bring more of those adverse circumstances into my life in an ever-increasing cycle. If I know who I am in Jesus, I will start to attract heaven into my life, and my circumstances will eventually bow to that reality that has already been birthed in my heart by faith.

PTSD no longer the issue

Circumstances can so pile up in our lives that they even cause physical illness. I have seen many illnesses healed because of inner-healing/deliverance. Eric is someone with whom I prayed who had such a servant's heart that he would not even acknowledge he had any problems at all. He actually was contacting me to pray with his brother who was also an amazing servant but was bedridden with illness and oppression. Eric's brother was a paramedic. Eric had been in the military, had been a police officer, and a firefighter. He apparently had a servant's heart.

While I was on the phone with him talking about his brother, the Holy Spirit kept telling me that Eric had problems. I would say to Eric, "I am going to pray with your brother but what is going on with you?" He would deflect and say, "I'm ok," and then would start talking about his brother again. The Holy Spirit would prompt me again to pray with Eric. He would deflect again and say, "I'm ok," and then would start talking about his brother again. The Holy Spirit once again said, "Ask him what is going on with him." Finally, I told Eric, "The Holy Spirit is wearing me out to pray with you. What is going on with you?"

He said, "When I was in the military I was struck by lighting, and I have also had a heat stroke. I have now been disabled for 12 years, I am depressed, and suicidal at times and it has really affected my marriage." He said, "I have PTSD." I later found out that when he left his house, his wife would push him around in a wheelchair. I said, "If that is okay with you then I would hate to see what it is like when you are not okay. Let's set up a time to pray together." He agreed, and we went through the first round of prayer. It was full on deliverance. We did no inner healing.

Instead we were focusing on getting off all the spirits that had attached through his years of being in the service and just being a man of action as a first responder. I later found out that he didn't believe that followers of Jesus could even have spirits attached to them. The second round of prayer that I did was another full-on deliverance. At one point, I prayed for the fire of the Holy Spirit to come down and burn up everything not of Him and the power of God hit Eric and knocked him out of his chair and onto the floor. One of the amazing parts about both sessions is that they were done over the phone. I heard Eric hit the floor and I heard him start speaking in tongues in a loud voice even though he did not believe in speaking in tongues.

It's amazing when God ambushes people and changes a lifelong theological belief in a second with an encounter with Him. I then prayed a PTSD healing prayer over Eric that I learned from a gentleman by the name of Dr. Mike Hutchings, who is a director with Global Awakening. Eric got up off the floor, free and completely healed. Eric also didn't believe that physical healing was for today. He went back to work after being disabled for 12 years and started going to the gym and working out again. The depression was gone, and so were the suicidal thoughts. The enemy had attacked his value through his circumstances and tried to take him out of the spiritual battle, but the enemy did not know the fighter that Eric was. He was willing to go through a prayer he didn't even believe in, and God rewarded him with healing and freedom.

How to win

One of the ways we defeat this pattern is to first recognize what is actually going on. We see that the enemy is trying to push the programmed buttons of the core lie to get us to respond with the established stronghold. This continues to reinforce it. But we also know that the Father's heart is postured to bless us and turn every attack of the enemy into a blessing.

Therefore, I pray in such a way that aligns my heart with His, and I give him the reason He is looking for to bless and prosper me. Spirits not only manifest on a person and cause strongholds of behavior, but they also create atmospheres over a person. Have you ever seen someone you didn't even know, and you wanted to reject them? You don't know anything about them, yet before you ever talk with them, your heart is postured to reject them. Why is that? It is because they have a spirit of rejection on them.

The spirit of rejection has gotten the person to come into agreement or express faith with the idea that they will be rejected and they invite rejection everywhere they go and with everyone they meet. There is a flashing demonic marquee over their souls in the spiritual realm that reads, "Reject me." I frequently ask Jesus to tear down the marker over the person's head in the spiritual realm and name that marker after the person has broken agreement with it. We are asking Jesus to create atmospheres over others that are consistent with who they are in Him.

Atmospheres vs. attacks

Atmospheres are another issue we will deal with in all the patterns but that can really become an issue in Pattern 3. Atmospheres are the result of upper-level spirits' having power and authority in an area that is large or small. Everything from homes to nations have an atmosphere. Atmospheres are created by agreements. The more people who are in agreement with a spirit, the more power and authority that spirit has and the stronger the atmosphere becomes. Generational lines have upper-level spirits that create atmospheres over those family lines. As we saw in Ephesians 6:12, our struggle is with different levels of spirits.

Upper-level and lower-level demons

I have done a deep dive into this passage, and there is a lot here. What I have found is that it's not necessary to have an in-depth knowledge of this passage to understand what is essential to be successful in fighting the war in which we find ourselves. The first thing we have to know is that we are no longer in a flesh and blood war like the Israelites in the Old Testament. Ours is a spiritual war, and to win, we have to send all our firepower in the direction of the right enemy. Our second takeaway is that all of the spirits we face can be categorized into two primary groups of upper-level and lower-level demonic spirits. We have to deal with each in two different ways. There is a Psalm that helps us understand the basics of how we exercise the authority Jesus has given us.

The heavens are the heavens of the Lord,
But the earth He has given to the sons of men. —*Psalm 115:16*

Heaven and Earth

Underneath His reign and rule, Jesus has given us the authority to rule over the things of the earth. But rule in the heavenly realm is reserved for Him. When we deal with an upper-level spirit, we ask Jesus to rebuke it since it is a second heaven level spirit. When we deal with a lower level spirit, we exercise the authority He has given us to rule on His behalf on the matters of the earth, and we command the spirit to go in Jesus' name since it is an earthly spirit. This is based on a deliverance protocol and is not a blueprint for intercessory prayer. There are two primary times you will deal with upper-level spirits. One is when you sense or feel atmospheres in small areas such as homes, churches, and buildings or regions such as towns, cities, states, and even nations. The other is when you deal with generational issues where these spirits establish atmospheres that create strongholds over generational bloodlines. This is a more comprehensive way to deal with generational spirits and is, again, a principal, not a law.

I have seen cases where generational issues were cleansed without going after the upper-level spirits. I have also seen cases where the generational issues were not cleansed without addressing the upper-level spirits. Can you deal with generational issues without dealing with upper-level spirits? In a word, I will say yes, but it may not work every time. Upper-level spirits literally take a couple of extra minutes in your protocol. I think it is worth the extra couple of minutes based on the results I have seen.

Discernment desired

The reason you feel or sense regional or even generational atmospheres is because the supernatural gift of discerning of spirits is operating in your life. That is a good thing even though it won't feel like it at times when atmospheres get heavy. If you are new at functioning in this gift, you will struggle to know whether it is an atmosphere or whether you have opened the door to a spirit. The Holy Spirit will help you to discern the difference. If it is an atmosphere, you just declare that you are a representative of the Kingdom of God, and the spirit does not set the atmosphere around you. Declare that Jesus is Lord of everything in and around your life, and any spirit that is trying to influence or enter your atmosphere will have to submit to the lordship of Jesus. Then ask Jesus to put a bubble of peace around you. You will feel an immediate shift in the atmosphere.

Generational victory

To deal with atmospheres over generational lines, you will repent on behalf of you and your generational lines for all the sins, iniquities, and transgressions that you name. Then, ask that the blood of Jesus cleanse you and your generational lines all the way back to Adam and forward. Next, ask Jesus to rebuke the upper-level spirits involved, and after this, command the lower level spirits to go in Jesus name. It is also wise to break all unholy soul ties with your generational lines before you command the spirits to go.

Generational atmospheres

The reason that I include addressing upper-level spirits in this book is that the Holy Spirit has shown me that upper-level spirits were involved almost every time I dealt with generational issues in creating atmospheres. That's why now, I just go after upper-level spirits every time there is a generational issue involved. I have seen it make a real difference in the people I pray with, and it is a much more comprehensive way to deal with generational issues and the resulting spiritual attachments.

Why would Paul tell us about the different ranks of spirits if we didn't need to know to how to deal with them in different ways? In 2 Peter 2, verses 10 to 12 explain that those who go against higher-level spirits without going through the proper order before the Lord, and it didn't go well for them.

"Daring, self-willed, they do not tremble when they revile angelic majesties, whereas angels who are greater in might and power do not bring a reviling judgment against them before the Lord. But these, like unreasoning animals, born as creatures of instinct to be captured and killed, reviling where they have no knowledge, will in the destruction of those creatures also be destroyed," —2 Peter 2:10-12

There's a better way to win

I have prayed with several people who went after upper-level spirits while interceding in regional warfare and seen the backlash that can come through presumptuous prayer. When I go against spirits that are creating atmospheres in generational lines, I ask the Lord to rebuke them, and I don't get into trouble that way.

Authority makes a difference

When dealing with atmospheres connected to property, it matters whether or not you have authority over the property. This occurs when you either own the property or have temporary custody, which means that someone in authority has given you permission to stay on their property or cleanse their property.

Mine altering experience

An example of what I am talking about occurred when I was asked to fly to another state and cleanse a mine on behalf of its new owner. We arrived the night before, and I woke up early to hear what the Holy Spirit wanted to tell me about the mine. As I prayed into what had power and authority over the mine, I heard that there had been unfair and unsafe mining practices, which had caused multiple deaths to occur over the years. I also heard that there had been a fire and that Wiccans had cursed the mine. When the owner met me for breakfast, I gave him the download of what I had heard. He researched it on the internet, and everything that I had heard that morning, was backed up except the Wiccan curse. That was not hard to believe since they worship creation and are known to curse anyone taking resources from the Earth.

Cursing in the house

The next day, we met at the house of one of the leaders of the company and I did a session with his wife. Toward the end of the session, the leader walked into the room to check on his wife, and I felt a heavy demonic presence. I asked the Holy Spirit what I was picking up on, and I heard the words "Africa" and "cursed object." I told him what I heard, and he ran out of the room, and I thought I had either offended him or freaked him out.

That night, several other people were in his house, two of whom did not believe in Jesus, and would be accompanying us in the mine the following day. We got into a long discussion about the war between the two kingdoms of light and darkness, and everyone seemed to be engaged. The leader spoke about the word I had given him earlier in the day. He shared that immediately after I had spoken, the Lord gave him a vision of a game he had brought back from Africa, and he threw it away. He said he felt an immediate shift in his house. He'd known something had been wrong in his home and he now knew why.

Atmospheric pressure

The next day, ten of us went into the mine and the two unbelievers accompanied us. As we went deeper and deeper into the mine, I was not sensing any demonic presence anywhere we went. As we started down the last corridor, about 3,000 feet into the mine, all of a sudden, I felt an extremely heavy atmosphere. It was one of the strongest presences I had ever experienced. I started praying under my breath in tongues and warring against the spirit trying to make me submit to his atmosphere and turf. We walked another 100 yards and the leader stopped and said that was where a couple of miners had died. I said that explained what I had been sensing over the last 100 yards. I told them about the heavy presence, and I could tell that was not what anyone wanted to hear 3,000 feet down in a dimly lit mine.

Fire in the hole

They nervously asked if I wanted to pray there, and I said we should continue to the end of the corridor. When we got to the end, I explained what I was about to do. I then repented on behalf of those who had gone before us for unfair and unsafe mining practices that had caused the death and devaluation of employees and anything else that had opened the door to the demonic and that had dishonored God in any way. I then canceled every curse that had been placed on the mine with the blood of Jesus and commanded every spirit not of the spirit of God to leave the mine in Jesus' name. Everyone physically felt that presence leave the mine. I then said, "Holy Spirit, we claim this mine as kingdom territory and we invite you to fill every square inch of it in Jesus' name." I have been where the presence of the Holy Spirit was thick, and I have never felt Him in an atmosphere more intense than how He showed up in the mine that day. One of the unbelievers was staring at me with huge eyes, and he said: "I have tingles all over my body, what is this?" I said, "it is the Holy Spirit." The young atheist walked up beside me and said: "Can I have your phone number? I think you could be a positive influence in my life."

Far-sighted

My wife and sister-in-law were back in our home city and were praying for us in the mine but they did not know when we were going into the mine. I got a text from them right as we exited the mine and they described what had just taken place. The text said that they had heard a huge explosion and saw several demons flying out of the top of the mine! They then saw the Holy Spirit sweep in carrying gold!

Power evangelism

I ended up leading both of the unbelievers to Jesus that night. Power evangelism, where kingdom power is demonstrated is the best way to do evangelism. I could have debated that atheist for 10 years and never seen breakthrough. One power encounter with the Holy Spirit, and he surrendered to King Jesus and was transferred from the Kingdom of Darkness to the Kingdom of Light.

Attacks bring blessing

One of the ways we defeat this pattern is first recognizing what is actually going on. We see that the enemy is trying to push the programmed buttons of the core lie to get us to respond by establishing and reinforcing the stronghold, but we also know that the Father's heart is postured to bless us and turn every attack of the enemy into a blessing. Therefore, I pray in such a way that aligns my heart with His, and I give him the reason He is looking for to bless and prosper me.

When I discern that the enemy is attacking me, I pray in the opposite spirit of what the enemy is trying to accomplish in me with the attack. If he is trying to motivate me by pushing my buttons through my wife, I will immediately forgive her and start praying to God to take this attack and use it to bless my wife and my marriage in a way that was not available before the attack. Let the attack bring about blessing. Sometimes I will get very specific about the blessings. Sometimes I will ask to lead someone to Jesus, sometimes I will ask for a healing. I am just looking for ways to make the attack cost the kingdom of darkness. You will be amazed at how quickly this shuts the mouth of the enemy and thwarts its attack.

Every attack of the enemy can actually become a gift to you. Every circumstance you overcome becomes a new area of freedom that expands the borders of your promised land. That new territory now becomes an area the enemy has lost control of and handed to you through defeat. It's a new part of your land, your inheritance that you just received. By faith, you are a son or daughter of Abraham, and the more you act like it, the greater your inheritance becomes.

"Therefore, be sure that it is those who are of faith who are sons of Abraham."
—*Galatians 3:7*

Own their gates

This qualifies you to receive the promises made to Abraham's offspring. One of the promises is that his offspring will own the gates of their enemies *(Gen. 22:17)*. That means every time you overcome a stronghold or circumstance, you now own that gate. A gate is a defensive weapon that keeps some people in and other people out.

When you own a gate, you, instead of the enemy, have the key. You get let out of what had you in bondage, and you are able to let others out with the same key.

Every time you give into a circumstance or an attack, you will have to face it again, and it will be stronger the next time. Every time you overcome, you are stronger than that enemy in that area, and you will eventually not have to face it anymore because you own that gate and have gained real authority and power over that enemy there.

When you posture your heart to align with heaven in this way and pray with this mindset, you have now become a hard target. The enemy has to make a calculated risk to attack you and now has to figure out if you are worth attacking since you know how to pray and turn every attack into promotion and blessing. This frees God to beat the devil with His own stick on your behalf.

Who God is to us in Pattern 3: **El Roi = The God Who Sees**

Hagar called God El Roi; this is the first time that name is used for God in the Bible. No other response was adequate when she encountered the God who sees in the midst of her desperate circumstances of being pregnant, homeless, alone, and broken in the desert without water. In an ancient twist on words, she said that she remained alive after seeing the One who sees. When we see the God who sees us in the midst of our desperation, we do much more than remain alive: We come alive. It's the very opposite of what the enemy tries to program our hearts to see as he fires a barrage of fiery missiles at our hearts through people and circumstances. As our eyes honestly see the God who sees, the shield of faith rises to extinguish those arrows before their tips, dipped in poisonous lies, can penetrate our hearts. The God who sees anxiously waits to answer the prayers of those who cry out to Him in their wilderness. The God who sees is desperate to remove our blindness to see Him instead of our desperation. The God who sees causes us to see ourselves, Him, and our circumstances in a way that only heaven can see.

Scripture: *"The Lord, the Lord God, compassionate and gracious, slow to anger, and abounding in lovingkindness and truth; who keeps lovingkindness for thousands, who forgives iniquity, transgression and sin; yet He will by no means leave the guilty unpunished, visiting the iniquity of fathers on the children and on the grandchildren to the third and fourth generations."* *—Exodus 34:6-7*

Tool: Supreme court of heaven

Activation:

- Ask Jesus to let you come before the courts of heaven. Pay attention to what you see as you enter the court, what you are wearing, whether Jesus is beside you, what the courtroom looks like, and if your adversary is present.
- Ask the Father to open your books and reveal every accusation the enemy is using in the court case against you to block your destiny.
- Write down what you hear. Repent of everything you hear on behalf of you and your generational lines. Matthew 5 tells us to agree with our accuser quickly so that we can be free of accusation.
- Ask that all of it be nailed to the cross and cleansed with the blood of Jesus all the way back to Adam and forward. Cut all unholy soul and spiritual ties with your generational lines and all sex partners outside of marriage including all the images of pornography.
- Command every spirit associated with the blocks to leave in Jesus' name. Continue to command until you sense that every spiritual attachment has gone.
- Ask for the Holy Spirit to fill you back up and to release your full destiny in Him.

JOSEPH PRAYER

Pattern 4:

Avoiding pain doesn't

We develop pain-avoiding strongholds to deal with the pain
of the core lie.

Joseph's Pattern 4: He sits alone in prison for a crime he didn't commit, in a country he didn't choose, with the enemy whispering in his ear that everyone had abandoned him including God. It finally seemed like the right time to take matters into his own hands and use his gift of dream interpretation as his crowbar on the door of his prison cell. Joseph wanted out and for a brief moment, cutting a deal seemed like the best way to accomplish it. Even though he had found favor everywhere he went, it still seemed like God had forgotten about him, maybe the cupbearer wouldn't. After all, the cupbearer was connected all the way up the ladder to Pharaoh himself. Maybe the cupbearer could take away the cup that Joseph had been drinking for way too many years.

"Only keep me in mind when it goes well with you, and please do me a kindness by mentioning me to Pharaoh and get me out of this house. For I was in fact kidnapped from the land of the Hebrews, and even here I have done nothing that they should have put me into the dungeon." — Genesis 40:14-15

Joseph's pain-avoiding stronghold: Use your gifts to prove that you matter and to get what you want or need.

Most of the idols of our hearts are strongholds fashioned with the tools of pain avoidance. Because our core lie enters at such an early age, we start trying to avoid the devaluing pain that accompanies it, almost immediately and without Jesus. We don't have the spiritual skills at that age to overcome the pain by partnering with Him. That reality causes us to avoid pain any way that works. The devil places us in the pit of our core lie and then hands us a shovel of pain avoidance and says, "Dig, and you will get out." In other words, he wounds us and then gives us the way to manage the pain. Pain avoiding strongholds are the result. The activity of digging with the shovel of pain avoidance feels much better than doing nothing. Some measure of success in reducing the pain level occurs, which creates an addiction to the shovel. Yet the pit of our insecurity just grows deeper and deeper with every shovel full of avoidance.

Wake up

Over time, we become subconscious masters at avoiding pain. At the same time, we remain entirely unaware of what we are actually participating in and with. I say subconscious because all of this occurs on a heart level and most people in the West are detached from their hearts. They are utterly unconscious of the war the enemy is waging inside of them. In fact, most of us don't realize we are assisting the enemy by being at war with ourselves. My friend, Chris, words this civil war of our hearts in a somewhat humorous way by describing his own season of Pattern 4: "I was a willing co-conspirator to my own demise." We are just unaware of our hearts' response to the enemy's attacks.

One of my most significant challenges in a session involves getting people out of their heads and re-connected to their hearts. God speaks to the heart with spiritual language because it brings revelation of the spiritual assault coming against our lives frequently through circumstances and people.

Pain floats

Current circumstances are just the right irritant poured into the boiling pot of your life causing your real issues to rise to the top. Running from your circumstances never makes them go away because, you aren't really running from the circumstances, you're actually running from yourself. You're the one the lies are all about, and core lies are the root cause of most of the pain. Running from the pain means running from lies you believe about yourself. Circumstances appear as the ever-narrowing walls of the alley you run down to avoid letting the Lord examine your heart and heal it. Wherever you go, there you are, and ultimately God is waiting for you at the end of the alley once you surrender.

Avoiding pain is painful

Because we were never meant to live with a devalued identity, disconnected from our gifting and destiny, the resulting insecurity forces us to do something to minimize the pain. We were meant to live as a daughter or son of the King, living out the words He prophesied over us in the womb. When that doesn't happen, the resulting pain causes us to develop patterns of pain-avoidance that turn into strongholds, inspired by the demonic realm. Those spirits, in a very targeted way, bring pain and trauma into our lives and then train us to minimize the pain through sinful strategies of pain-avoidance, management, and retaliation.

Most of the sin in our lives is a direct result of coping with the lie-based pain we manage instead of surrendering it to Jesus. He literally died to heal us and set us free. Very few of us ever connect the dots that these strongholds have actually resulted from avoiding the pain of believing lies. We can't see it, even though the concept is described, as we have already seen, in 2 Corinthians 10:4-5. God intends for us to use His divinely powerful weapons to destroy these lies and blow up the pain-avoiding strongholds that are built on their foundation.

Being pain-avoiding creatures makes it incredibly challenging to get to the root of our issues. We run from pain instead of staring it down. We fail to realize that with all the power and backing of heaven, walls of self-protection will fall just like those in Jericho. They will fall when we invite Jesus to join us in circling those walls with shouts of agreement with His truths. If our lies get destroyed and our pain gets healed, we won't need a pain-avoiding strategy anymore.

Root, not fruit

Destroying the root lies breaks down the walls of behaviors and patterns that result in demonically-inhabited fortresses. When the need to avoid pain goes away, we are left with merely a habit. We can break a habit but have an almost impossible task to overcome with a soul that needs to self-medicate. Demonic spirits remain attached to addictive behaviors unless we deal with the root lies and cast out the spirits attached to the lies. You can't counsel a demon out, and you can't cast out your will. There is a place for Bible study, counseling, and prayer. There is also a place for utilizing the authority and power of Jesus to drive out the demonic tormentors the way that He did.

We run to careers, money, possessions, religion, relationships, self-help books, and a host of other ways to medicate our pain. We go after our pain-avoiding drug of choice in the same way the severely drug-addicted throw their lives away chasing the next high. It seems that drug addiction is much more easily recognized self-medicating activity. Those with more socially acceptable pain-avoiding strategies have a much harder time acknowledging and owning their addiction.

Strongholds cause blindness

We like our strongholds but judge other strongholds that appear less desirable to us. A stronghold is a stronghold. Not a single one advances us on the path of destiny. In God's economy, without faith it is impossible to please Him. Any pain-avoiding strategy that is not in lockstep with Jesus will not set us free from the pain we are trying to avoid. It may temporarily give us relief, but these sin vacations become very costly trips to take. Lost destinies and squandering inheritance is all they add up to in the long run. I made a tweak to a famous saying which makes it hit a little closer to the heart of the issue we are discussing.

"Watch your feelings; they express your beliefs;
watch your beliefs; they monitor thoughts;
watch your thoughts; they become words;
watch your words; they become actions;
watch your actions; they become habits;
watch your habits; they become character;
watch your character; for it becomes your destiny."

It's not your personality

We can't afford to use the coping strategy, "That's my personality" as the carpet we sweep under the distorted views of ourselves. Who you really are can only be seen through the eyes of the Father because He is the only one that spoke your true self into being while you were in the womb. Without looking through His eyes, we have a distorted view of ourselves. It's reminiscent of the apps on our phones that maintain just enough of our image to still look like us yet distort our faces into twisted versions of what we really look like. That's a humorous image on a phone, and not so funny when it represents your life.

These comic distortions symbolize the areas of our soul that the enemy has molded us like clay into hideous caricatures of our true self. The more we agree with this false image of ourselves the more leverage the enemy has to reinforce this false identity through people and circumstances. Cinderella is everyone's story. Will you believe the pursuit and affection of your prince Jesus and put on the slippers of your destiny with Him? Or will you give into the distortions of the lies perpetuated by the evil, demonic, stepsisters? The latter will cause you to stay locked away in the basement of your soul serving all their evil wishes.

Painful performance

Joe's example reveals how these distorted views of self, lead to strongholds in the soul. The enemy put the core lie that he was not good enough in his heart when he was six. When I got him to ask Jesus to reveal how he had coped with this lie his whole life, he started to weep because he began to see how his whole life was affected by this lie. It came in through a school incident when he was called on for an answer and felt exposed as not being smart enough when he missed the answer in front of the whole class. It was a such devastating moment to him as a six-year-old that the lie got implanted in his heart that he wasn't good enough. As we prayed, the realization hit him that he had spent the rest of his life trying to prove, in his own strength, that he was good enough.

He started performing for others, looking for their approval. He realized he had placed God's stamp of approval on all his activities by claiming he was doing everything motivated by excellence. After all, God wants us to do things with excellence right? As he progressed in life and got really good at performing, he became focused on the end result and not the process. He began to strive and push aggressively to always come out on top. He slowly started to shift from the gateway drug of people-pleasing to the harder drug of winning. He started stepping on people and becoming progressively more performance driven, and it pushed him to the top and into a lonely place.

He had been a Christian most of his life and not just a Sunday morning one either. When I prayed with him, he was in his late 60's and had been the top performing salesman of every job he had ever had. He had done a lot of amazing things for the kingdom as well. He had written Christian books, generously given of his wealth, time, and talents. He had traveled the world, opened his house up to meetings, speakers and guests, all for the Kingdom of God. Joe is an excellent example of someone whom God has used in powerful ways, yet there was a part of his heart still functioning out of a core lie. He had been coping with it in ways that he had been blind to his whole life. He couldn't see the reason he was so driven was because he had been trying to prove that six-year-old boy really was good enough for over sixty years. His own efforts to fix himself had not worked, but one moment with Jesus changed everything in his heart, when Jesus removed the lens of that lie.

It's not all bad

Core lies don't always ruin a whole life as in Joe's case. He had accomplished amazing things in his life led by the Holy Spirit. But there was a lot of it that had passed through the lens of proving he was good enough, which had tainted it. That part had caused him to strive and isolate, burning through a couple of marriages in the process. As that revelation hit him on a heart level and he wept, he said, "I feel like my whole life has been a waste." I had him ask Jesus if that was a true statement. Jesus answered back with an emphatic "absolutely not!" and began to walk Joe through all the things he had done in partnership with Him. Jesus also spoke into him a name of endearment that I will keep between Joe and Jesus that really wrecked him. Jesus exposed the core lie that day because He didn't want it to steal from Joe anymore. Jesus desperately loved him and expressed it to him that day. He was wanting to set Joe free from pain-avoiding strongholds that had motivated Joe for over sixty years. He just wanted all of Joe's heart. He doesn't want to share His bride with any lesser lovers.

Heart knowledge

The collective worldview we share as Americans adds to the fog of war. We are an information-based society. We are sold out to the ancient Greek mindset of reason. We place a high value on intellect, education, and rational thought with little to no emphasis on connection to heart knowledge. Jesus didn't recite the greatest commandment as loving God only with all your mind; He included loving God with all your heart, soul, and mind. I find it interesting that, in the order He gave, mind shows up last.

God wants every part of us engaged with Him, yet many of us limit His access to only our left brain. If the heart and soul don't get engaged, we will wonder why we don't feel the love of God yet have information in our head that claims He loves us. We wonder why we have no power and why the supernatural realm doesn't manifest as part of lives. The sad part comes when we no longer care as we gravitate toward a theology that helps explain it away. We wonder why few develop an interest in our version of Christianity and why our churches are dying as a result. If we don't passionately engage our hearts in our beliefs, we know it, and everyone around us knows it too. With only our head engaged, we are probably involved in religion over relationship, and that deadly activity never expresses the abundant life Jesus promised.

True religion isn't religious

Religious spirits create one of the biggest strongholds in the church where we strive to perform without admitting we are broken and invite Jesus to heal our brokenness. We prefer looking good over being good. We are Martha instead of Mary. Jesus was unimpressed with all of Martha's striving and said Mary went after what was important. Sitting at His feet, in deep communion with Him, that's the main thing Jesus is after, and it's the main thing that will heal our broken hearts *(Lk. 10:38-42)*. Many people will let Jesus into their head but will never expose their heart to Him. God words it this way through the prophet Isaiah:

"Render the hearts of this people insensitive, Their ears dull, And their eyes dim. Otherwise, they might see with their eyes, Hear with their ears, Understand with their hearts, And return and be healed." —Isaiah 6:10

Spiritual eyes and ears

Isaiah spoke about people who listen with physical ears but not with spiritual ears. They sought information, not revelation. They checked the box of learning a topic and were now in danger of thinking they knew it because they had heard the information about it. That activity numbs the heart and increasingly closes off the spirit to receiving revelation from the Holy Spirit. A numbed out heart will find stimulation somehow and usually through sin since it fails to surrender to intimacy with Jesus. His word either softens the heart or hardens it, but it never returns void. A hard heart gets hardened further by listening to the word without responding to it. When Jesus spoke to the woman at the well, He cried out for those who will worship in spirit and in truth *(Jn. 4:23)*. We need two legs to stand on for spiritual wholeness. We need our head and our hearts intimately connected to Jesus through the Holy Spirit.

Know Him or know about Him

Our left brain based society has so affected the church that we think the solution to all of our spiritual issues will be resolved with more information. This mindset pushes us into a very subjective, intellectual corner where we are afraid of being deceived. The whole time we remain there we are being entirely deceived by being disconnected from our hearts. We think that our minds will prevent us from being deceived. There are scores of men and women with the IQ of a genius who couldn't be any more deceived in spiritual matters. Many times from this intellectual corner, we get boxed into thinking that we can figure out all of our issues and fix them ourselves. If our number one fear is being deceived, we already are. The goal of Christianity is not to avoid deception and counterfeits as much as it is to intimately know the real thing— Jesus. If we intimately know Him, deceiving us becomes a real challenge for the enemy to pull off. We don't have to chase every new tactic of the enemy; if we just intimately know Jesus, then the counterfeits will blatantly stand out to us.

Satan loves religion

Religion manifests as the pain-avoiding stronghold of choice for the enemy. It maximizes the reach and damage of someone living disconnected from the truth like none other. It is more addictive than any drug, and looks like it has God's stamp of approval on it, which makes it certainly more socially acceptable. Religious activity always seems so reasonable to the person involved in it, but it has a demonic spirit behind it. And the religious spirit is one of the worst we have to deal with. There were two divisive spirits Jesus warned us about; the leaven of Herod—political spirit— and the leaven of the Pharisees—religious spirit *(Mk. 8:15)*.

What both spirits have in common is the coping strategy of being right. It's how they divide. Someone who was infected with false information by a person in authority frequently will partner with one or both of these spirits to cope with the pain. A political spirit doesn't care which party you choose as long as you decide to divide over being right. The religious spirit doesn't care which flavor of religion you choose, as long as you're more interested in being right than showing the love of Jesus.

Jesus offends the religious

Jesus spent much of His day offending the religious spirit. He could heal any day of the week He wanted but frequently chose the Jewish Sabbath. This was to expose the religious death grip the religious spirit had on the hearts of the Jewish people of His day. Jesus would radically heal someone of a lifelong illness, and instead of celebrating, the religious were ready to kill Jesus over which day of the week He did it on. That exposes how messed up our heart can get when bitten with the spirit of religion. It completely disconnects our hearts from the loving heart of the Father, and He will be perceived as a taskmaster instead of Abba. Jesus claimed to be the visible representative of the Father's heart of compassion to those who knew they needed it. Have you ever realized that it was the Father who actually told Jesus to heal on the Sabbath? Jesus said He only did what He saw the Father doing.

Religion numbs the heart

The religious spirit anesthetizes us from the tenderness and goodness of the love of God while at the same time convincing us that the one thing that will cure the insecure ache in our heart is to be right. It then assures us that if we learn from the right person, that went to the right seminary, that has the correct number of degrees after their name, we will be right. We will then be able to win every theological debate, and cause the insecurity to whither and finally go away. As we get so deeply invested in our addiction to being right, we can no longer detect that our heart has grown harder and more calloused with every book, debate, and podcast.

Right vs. relationship

The religious person values rightness over relationship every time. They're harsh, critical, judgmental, angry, and blind. They can't see that the fact-gathering activity they are involved in is the furthermost thing from expressing the tender heart of the Father. Religion places a high value on conformity and right doctrine since doctrine is on the throne of their life instead of Jesus. This is the very group that Jesus spoke to when he said, *"You search the Scriptures because you think that in them you have eternal life; it is these that testify about Me."* —*John 5:39*

Religious "right doctrine" is actually a perversion of unity. In fact, many times, where you find the religious spirit you will find devaluing and disconnection from the Holy Spirit. The reason is that the Holy Spirit is the only way we will ever have unity. He is the Spirit of unity. The religious spirit has to discredit His activity to gain control, because the Spirit of truth will expose him and prevent division. Skepticism, fear, and control are some of his favorite side-effects to enforce a religious mindset.

If the church is trying to find unity in right doctrine, it will never happen. Finding unity in doctrine is impossible because we are all supposed to be growing, and as we do our doctrines will be expanding and adjusting as the Holy Spirit gives us more insight.

Targets not dominos

When I first got saved, I had a "domino theology." I believed that, if any of my dominos fell, they all would fall. This made me get into "right fights," defending the most obscure doctrine as if my salvation depended on it; because, in my heart, it did. As my relationship with God has deepened, along with a few supernatural encounters with the Holy Spirit along the way, and I now have a "target theology."

There are a few things in my bullseye that I am willing to die over, and the more mature I get, the fewer things there are in my bullseye. The further you get away from the bullseye, the more I can get into a healthy passionate debate with you and end up disagreeing but still respect you and love you as a brother or sister in Christ. This is because theology is no longer a coping strategy for a heart wounded by religion and bad theology. Jesus now sits on the throne; I don't need you to agree with me for me to be OK with my beliefs, and it makes all the difference in the world. Some of my most significant changes have been because of a healthy debate when I disagreed with someone, forcing me to have to go back and reassess what I thought was true. It has changed me on more than one occasion. In whom I believe never changes. What I believe is continuously evolving.

Love unifies

That is why we can only find unity in love. Love is the umbrella we can all sit under and disagree on doctrine in different seasons of growth and still remain in unity. We have to provide a safe place to skin our doctrinal knees and still stay in unity. Jesus didn't say that if you believe the same thing the world will know you are my disciple. He said if you love one another the world will know. Right doctrine too often kicks love to the curb in order to park in the right spot.

This is not advocating to negate standards or core beliefs which make us uniquely Christian. If you don't believe in the death, burial, and resurrection of Jesus, you are not a Christian and not in a relationship with Jesus, period. If you don't believe Jesus is the only way to the Father, you are not a Christian. There are a few core beliefs we have to draw a line in the sand over, but those are a far cry from dividing over some of the minor, doctrinal, non-critical issues the church has divided over for centuries.

Doctrinal coping strategies

The reason we divide over doctrine is that it can actually be a coping strategy for not having to expose the pain in our hearts to Jesus and those we are in community with. As long as I know about God, I don't have to be exposed to that messy business of knowing God and being known by Him. It's what Paul described as holding to a form of godliness although denying its power. The Holy Spirit is the spirit of truth and unity, and any pursuit of truth apart from Him will never produce unity, love, or true revelation. This is at the heart of the lack of unity in the church. The focus is not on the love of Jesus or the power of the Holy Spirit.

Religion has many faces

Religious strongholds express themselves in many more ways when you get exposed to other faiths outside of the U.S. I was in another country on a trip praying with people and watching Jesus perform miracles through healing and deliverance. One morning, I got about eight words of knowledge before I went to speak at the church we were ministering in, and I released all but one and saw all seven words of knowledge get healed in the various people that came forward for prayer. The one that I held back was for a woman who was barren that wanted a child. I didn't really know why I held it back. I even felt like I had been disobedient by keeping it back.

That night we were at someone's house who had invited several Hindus over to receive prayer. My friends who invited me and paid for my trip had been pouring into this country for over 10 years and had encouraged me to go with them on this trip. When we entered the house, my friend looked at me and said, "You know that word you held back, she's here tonight." Sure enough, the very last person that came forward for prayer was a lady who said: "I have not been able to have a child for over seven years." We all got excited because we had been watching Jesus heal everything He had given me words for that trip. We prayed for her to get pregnant.

Jesus is the only way

We later found out that she had gotten pregnant not long after we prayed. She had believed in Jesus before we met her, but after she got pregnant, she went back to worshiping the Hindu gods, maybe as some kind of insurance. Within a few months, she miscarried that baby. The religious idolatry she had come out of seemed to be too much of a stronghold to let go of, even in the face of a miracle of Jesus. I am not suggesting that God caused her miscarriage. I am suggesting when we place ourselves under the control of the false god's we worship we suffer under their cruel intentions. In this case, they certainly did not want a miracle of God to be born. She is now coming back to church, and the pastor has assured her that God has forgiven her and welcomes her back.

"I am the Lord, that is My name;
I will not give My glory to another,
Nor My praise to graven images. —Isaiah 42:8

Soul triggers

Sometimes the stronghold created by pain-avoidance inside each one of us becomes so ingrained that it grows into a soul reflex, like a doctor hitting our knee with a hammer to test our physical reflexes. When we have been programed by pain over a lifetime, without healing, we develop these soul reflexes or triggers. They are connected to the suffering of our core lies and one whack with the hammer of life, and we reflexively kick with our souls' programmed self-defensive response.

I watch people deflect, avoid and dance if I start getting anywhere close to their pain in a session. It is an instinct of the heart not to let anyone touch the pain. The problem with pain is that it cannot be healed if Jesus doesn't have the access needed to reach in with His healing touch. As long as we avoid, stuff, hide, and compartmentalize the pain, it won't be healed. Pain-avoiding strategies, many times, are directly linked to the core lie because it is the primary source of most of the pain. Let life press on the core lie, and you will find out quickly what the pain-avoiding strongholds are.

Hand it to Him

If we will turn this pain over to Jesus, He promises healing, freedom, and mending of our broken hearts. Wouldn't you have loved to be sitting in His hometown synagogue that day when He walked in the door, recorded in Luke 4? They handed Him the scroll of Isaiah, and He turned to Isaiah 61 and started to read;

"The Spirit of the Lord God is upon me,
Because the Lord has anointed me
To bring good news to the afflicted;
He has sent me to bind up the brokenhearted,
To proclaim liberty to captives
And freedom to prisoners;
To proclaim the favorable year of the Lord
And the day of vengeance of our God;" —Isaiah 61:1-2

He sat down, and everyone in the room knew that it was a mic drop moment. But Jesus added this, He said, "Today this scripture has been fulfilled in your hearing." That was a stunning statement that ultimately led to the religious trying to throw Him off of a cliff. He was claiming to be the one that Isaiah had written about some 600 years before that day. But the way the people initially responded was with their jaw in their lap, because they could feel the Holy Spirit's anointing on those words. Jesus came to bring good news to the afflicted, bind up broken hearts, set captives and prisoners free of their lie-based pain, and declare that every day is a jubilee day with Jesus, a day of freedom, a day to crawl out of the pit.

When we let go of our strongholds, push through the crowd of public opinion, and grab hold of the hem of His garment, healing, deliverance, and freedom will pour over us like the oil of gladness Isaiah talks about in the verses that directly follow the ones Jesus quoted in the synagogue that day.

Just telling someone to give up their pain-avoiding strongholds without showing them the lie behind it and helping them encounter Jesus in a way that replaces it, will never work. If it were that easy, we could start clearing the jails out tomorrow with the right message of "Just stop it." The jails are filled with those who were already living in the spiritual prison of pain-avoidance long before they were sentenced to physical imprisonment. Jesus promised to save, heal and deliver anyone that will surrender and let Him in.

Logan lays it down

Logan is someone who came to me with a pain-avoiding stronghold of alcohol abuse. He came to me because I had prayed with his girlfriend and she had experienced some freedom from the prayer. Enough freedom to tell him that he had to pursue getting free from abusing alcohol or she was moving on.

Since she was a believer in Jesus, I had assumed he was too, yet I was prompted to ask him where he was at with Jesus when he came to pray with me. He said, "Oh I'm an atheist." I said, "Ok, but you do realize that I am not a counselor, I am a prayer minister and prayer is all that I've got to offer? If that's not what you want, I can't offer you anything else." He said, "I have come to a place where I recognize a higher being of some kind." I said, "Well then you are not an atheist you are agnostic. You think there might be a higher power, but you haven't cared enough to find out which one." He said, "Yes that describes me and one of the main reasons I haven't pursued it is because I have never felt God. He is just not real to me."

I said, "I will pray with you, and I won't try to convert you, but one of the persons we are going to pray to is Jesus. Are you okay with that?" He said, "Yes." I said, "And if you are going to pray with me, you are going to at least be honest about who Jesus claimed to be. He will not allow you to lump Him in with all the other gods. He claimed to be the only way to the Father. You don't have to believe it for me to pray with you, but you have to acknowledge that was His claim."

I never require someone to believe in Jesus before I pray with them because I know what will happen if they agree to let me pray with them in a session. They will come to know Jesus and receive Him as Lord and savior. It has happened every time an unbeliever comes for a prayer session. I have lost count of the number of people that have gotten saved during a prayer session with me. Logan agreed, and I led him through forgiveness of everyone the Holy Spirit was showing him that he needed to forgive. He was hearing the voice of God on an amazing level. I then had him ask the Father if there was anything untrue he believed about Him. Logan saw a vision of the sun. I asked him what that meant to him, and he said, "I guess it's the way I view God as a distant thing." I said, "He is telling you that is not true what do you want to do about it."

He repented of believing God was a distant thing. Then he said "As I was repenting, I realized that even though the sun is distant, you can still feel its warmth on earth." He then looked at me with a stunned look on his face and said, "Oh my God, I feel heat all over my body." I knew he was being touched with the presence of the Holy Spirit who sometimes manifests with heat. I got up and laid hands on him and asked the Holy Spirit to touch him with fire and he broke out sweating on his forehead and started to shake and tremble under the power of the Holy Spirit. I then asked Jesus to touch every love deficit in his heart, and he began to weep uncontrollably. I sat back down and watched him get wrecked with the love of Jesus and the fire of the Holy Spirit for about 15 minutes. When he looked up I said, "You now know Jesus is real. Are you ready to hear about him? He said "Yes." I led him through the gospel, and he received Jesus.

Pain-avoiding gifts

Perhaps the most subtle of all pain-avoiding strongholds is the one Joseph used. We can use our supernatural gifting in manipulative ways. Joseph used his gifts of dream interpretation and leadership to gain the attention of those in charge to get what he wanted.

"Only keep me in mind when it goes well with you, and please do me a kindness by mentioning me to Pharaoh and get me out of this house." —Genesis 40:14

It may not be evident to you by the way the above text is worded but is what Joseph did any different than someone trying to gain notoriety through what they are doing for God? Joseph wanted Pharaoh to know about him so that he could get what he wanted, which was to get out of prison. He ignored going through God, and it cost him a couple of more years in the pit.

Nothing speaks to our performance-based hearts like using our gifting as proof that God values us and approves of us. This attitude is so counterproductive to what God intends His gifts to be used for that Paul dedicated a whole chapter to it, right in the middle of teaching on the supernatural gifts of the Holy Spirit. In 1 Corinthians 13, Paul goes through how worthless to God the activity surrounding any of the supernatural gifts becomes if detached from love. People with gifting greater than the level of love they carry in their hearts can do a lot of damage. This heart posture will use the gifts and the people they are exercising the gifts on as novocaine applied to the devaluing pain of their core lie.

Paul gives us the key to holding it all in balance at the beginning of chapter 14, which directly follows the chapter on love as he declares: "Pursue love, and earnestly desire the gifts." Love is what we are told to pursue, not the gifts. We are told to desire the gifts. The level of our pursuit of love will determine the level of outpouring of the gifts that we can handle.

Anytime we use the gifts to make us feel valued or loved, the enemy is perverting them from their original intent. If we have our value as a settled issue with Jesus, we will be able to function in our gifts freely and at full capacity. God will frequently ask us to lay our gifts on the altar, as He did Joseph, to purify those gifts so that God can eventually hand them back to us for our uncorrupted use. When our heart is free of value-seeking from the gifts, we will function in true Holy Spirit power, and those we are ministering to will be significantly impacted by the kingdom. We won't be guilty of using people as our pain-avoiding strategy to determine how much God values us.

You can't fix you

David had a fantastic insight into inner healing in Psalm 139:23-24. In this psalm, he asks God to search his heart and show him any way of pain, or any hurtful way in him. He recognized that he could not fix himself or even self-diagnose his issues through his intellect. David acknowledges that only God truly knew his heart. He realizes that hurt people, hurt people, but it is not their brokenness that is hurting everyone around them. It's the way they are coping with their brokenness that wreaks havoc on the people and circumstances in their lives. It's the demonic strongholds they are functioning in that does the real damage.

Running from our pain doesn't work. It delays our healing and increases our time in the pit. The clock is ticking on our destiny, gifts, and calling; we are not guaranteed another day on this Earth. You only get one shot at this life. I expect that many of our conversations in heaven will be about the war stories and all the miraculous ways that God showed up for us and all the people we interacted with. What happens today doesn't just affect tomorrow, it affects your eternity.

Enjoy the full gospel

To go to heaven is as simple as trusting in the death, burial, and resurrection of Jesus *(1 Cor. 15:1-4)*. But the gospel is so much more than getting to go to heaven one day, even though that in and of itself is amazing. God wants to bring heaven to Earth right now through you. Will you unconditionally surrender to Jesus and let Him heal your heart and empower you to step into your destiny? Then you can stop burning through years in a pit where you don't belong, clinging to a shovel that doesn't fit your hand, digging a deeper hole to crawl out of with every day you spend there. Abundant life awaits you outside the pit. There is a great cloud of witnesses cheering you on and longing to see what choices you will make today. If they could speak, they would tell you that today is not just another day. It carries eternal significance.

Who God is to us in Pattern 4: **Yahweh Shalom = The Lord is peace**
Gideon encountered the pre-incarnate Jesus in the form of the Angel of the Lord when he was hiding in the wine press from his enemies. The encounter marked him for the rest of his life, and he built an altar

to Him in response and named it, 'The Lord is Peace' *(Judg. 6:24)*. He encountered the Prince of Peace, and it unlocked something inside of him that had been in hiding his entire life. Gideon had been a coward, hiding from his enemies for years but one encounter with the Prince of Peace transformed him into his true identity as a mighty warrior. There is a great irony here that an encounter with peace unleashed a warrior on Israel's enemies. Gideon received what we need most in Pattern 4; an encounter with Jesus. His presence is the only thing that will stop us from chasing the false peace obtained through our pain-avoiding strongholds. The pain of the core lie can cause us to become cowards and hide in the strongholds created by our enemy.

Only Jesus can remove the ache of insecurity that has us wasting our destinies in the arms of lesser lovers. Pain-avoiding strongholds fall like the walls of Jericho when Jesus joins us on that 7th lap around the wall, shouting in agreement with Him that there is no longer any place for Jerichos in our hearts. Peace is the currency of heaven, and peace is what God uses to crush the head of the lie-spitting serpent He places underneath our feet *(Rom. 16:20)*. The enemy has no answer for peace, and we have no substitute for it because peace has a name, and His name is Jesus.

Scripture: *"Where can I go from Your Spirit?*
Or where can I flee from Your presence?
If I ascend to heaven, You are there;
If I make my bed in Sheol, behold, You are there.
If I take the wings of the dawn,
If I dwell in the remotest part of the sea,
Even there Your hand will lead me,
And Your right hand will lay hold of me." —*Psalm 139:7-10*

Tool: Lofty things (Exposes the lies raised up against the knowledge of God).

Activation:

- Ask Jesus to show you where He wants to meet with you.
- Ask Jesus to invite your original self (who you were originally created to be).
- Pay attention to what you look like and what you are wearing.
- Ask Jesus what each thing represented means.
- Ask Jesus what the core lie is that you believe about Him.
- Ask Him what patterns in your life were programed with that lie.
- Hand Him the lie and ask Him what He is replacing it with.
- Ask Him to take original self before the Father.
- Ask the Father what the core lie is that you believe about Him.
- Ask Him what patterns in your life were programed with that lie.
- Hand Him the lie and ask Him what He is replacing it with.
- Write down everything He shows you.

Pattern 5:

God trips us to keep us from falling

God allows us to be in circumstances that apply pressure on our pain-avoiding strongholds.

Joseph's Pattern 5: The very thing Joseph needed was the last thing he or anyone else would want: more unjust prison time. God caused the cupbearer to totally forget about Joseph. That caused Joseph to sit in prison for two more years. There were some things he could only learn in prison. One of them was not to use his gift to manipulate people and circumstances to get what he wanted or even needed. If God had allowed Joseph to get out of prison through using his gift like that, it would have been corruptible the rest of his life. The world stage God was about to place Joseph on required him and his gifts to function in incorruptible purity. Joseph was about to hold the salvation of all of humanity in the palm of his hand. He would go on to accurately interpret Pharaoh's dream about the coming famine, using godly wisdom to store up food, and save the known world from starvation. The Hebrews came to Egypt and were saved from certain death through starvation. Jesus would eventually come through the rescued Hebrew line. Without Joseph functioning in that role with integrity, the Hebrew line would have ended with Joseph. Big jobs require big, pure hearts.

"Thus it came about on the third day, which was Pharaoh's birthday, that he made a feast for all his servants; and he lifted up the head of the chief cupbearer and the head of the chief baker among his servants. He restored the chief cupbearer to his office, and he put the cup into Pharaoh's hand; but he hanged the chief baker, just as Joseph had interpreted to them. Yet the chief cupbearer did not remember Joseph but forgot him." — Genesis 40:20-23

Pressure on Joseph's stronghold: Two more years spent in prison.

Joseph's truth: I can't use my gifting to get what I want or achieve notoriety with leaders.

You were never meant to live in a pit. When you spend time in one, everything inside of you screams, "I don't belong here!" Being deeply invested in your core lie and the resulting strongholds forces the hand of God. He either leads you into or leaves you in circumstances that apply pressure on how you cope with your core lie apart from Him. He uses the pit to break you of all desire, compatibility, and compromise with your lies and strongholds. His passion for moving you out of the pit and into your destiny demands it. This pressure is intended to propel you out of the pit of your core lie and into the purpose for which you were born. Life outside the pit will persuade you to lay down your coping shovel because there will no longer be anything to dig above ground.

He's chasing you, turn around

The relentless love God shared with you in the womb won't let you be stolen away from Him by lesser lovers. None of us can fully inherit the Kingdom, even if we are saved, while living in the pit of our core lie, shoveling the pain with our coping strategy. That activity only causes the pit to grow deeper and broader with every shovel full of coping as another day of destiny ticks by.

To help us lose our ability to cope apart from Him, He will let it rain in the pit, get really hot in the pit, and let us hit rocks with our shovel in the pit. In other words, if you choose to cope with the devaluing insecurity of your heart apart from Jesus, you will spend a large portion of your life in a pit without understanding why nothing you try works.

You can actually shorten your time in the pit if you recognize the purpose of it. He's leading us to our Gethsemane. The place where we sweat drops of blood in anticipation of the death that lies ahead. But it's the only place that causes resurrection; it is the place in our journey where the road narrows, and there are no more exits. It's our time when "Satan asks to sift us like wheat." It's the time you endure after you have been anointed king and the current king throws spears at your head in a demonic, jealous rage, yet you refuse to strike back or say anything against him. *(1 Sam. 18:10-11)*

Brokenness puts us back together

You become the broken jar that releases the pure, nard perfume that fills the room with the fragrance of what has been growing inside of you ever since you met Jesus. *(Mk. 14:3-9)* That aroma causes the release of the sweet scent of Jesus to get everyone around you drunk with the smell. That's the day when angels roll back the stones in your life that have been blocking your resurrection from being released. That's the day you walk out of the tomb of your core lie so that everyone sees Jesus manifesting His resurrected life through yours. In that place, God hems us in on all sides to get us searching for the truth. Freedom is birthed as a direct result of the embrace when we come into agreement with truth. A raw embrace with God happens in the pit like in no other place.

Fight or flight?

Confusion usually accompanies the pit. Do we fight, surrender, or persevere? The answer to that question is often yes. If we are smart, we don't want to fight against God's intentions for us in the pit, but at the same time, we don't want to give in to an attack by the enemy, and we know that we have to persevere. Sometimes, fighting prolongs our prison time. Sometimes, giving up provides the enemy with a stronger foothold in our hearts. Sometimes persevering without fighting costs us. We become painfully aware of the trench warfare in which we are engaged, and at that point, the heavens can seem to be made of brass in response to our Psalmic cries.

So how do we know, at any given moment, whether to fight, surrender, or persevere? Only the Holy Spirit can reveal to us the right response. A heart postured to stay close to Him won't fight when surrender is needed and won't surrender when we need to fight. Staying close to Him will cause us to always be able to persevere. He will give us the answers we need at the right time. Many times all three are required at the same time because the enemy will never miss an opportunity to sell us into slavery while we are in the pit.

Humility is a weapon

True humility becomes a key and a weapon in the pit. God gives grace to the humble, but He resists the proud. When the demonic punches us in the face, we instinctively raise up the shield of pride to block the next punch. Don't ever expect fairness in the pit and don't look for many people to understand your unique pit. Be wary of advice in the pit, especially from those who have never been in the pit. The pat religious answers will come your way with chapter and verse. Remember Job's buddies (*Job 4-37*)? The enemy will tell that you are alone and that you have missed it because God has abandoned you. It's you against the world, but all of that is a lie. God will never be closer to you than He is in the pit.

"So I say to you, ask, and it will be given to you; seek, and you will find; knock, and it will be opened to you." —Luke 11:9

Surrender vs. giving up

There is a big difference between surrendering and giving up. The enemy wants you to give up, especially if you call it surrender. God wants true, unconditional surrender. It's been His ultimate desire for you since the day you came to know Jesus. Surrender keeps our hearts tender and trusting toward God and people while at the same time lays down all of our ability to cope with or prevent pain. The most exposed we will ever be will happen the day we let Jesus all the way into the most vulnerable, wounded, deceived parts of our heart. Giving up is throwing in the towel. Surrender is handing Him the towel to clean up with after He performs open heart surgery on us.

Everyone gets time in the pit

We will never fully step into our destiny without the pressures of the pit. Gold gets purified, pearls get made, gifts get refined, hearts resurrect, and destinies come alive. This womb of the pit births both ministries and monsters. It will make you or break you, some dreams will die and some will resurrect. You certainly won't come out of the pit the same way you went into it.

Upgrade follows surrender

Exiting the pit will temporarily cost you gifting and destiny. You will have to fully surrender them on the altar with the expectation of picking them back up one day once everything is in order. You can find this requirement throughout Scripture. David was anointed king and laid that anointing on the altar for 13 years before he became king. Paul was dramatically called to be an apostle and went into the wilderness for 13 years before he stepped into his destiny. Joseph was called to be a world leader and went to Egypt for 13 years before he sat on the throne. Abraham laid Isaac on the altar when Isaac was somewhere between 18 and 20 years old. Jesus was asked to lay His life on the altar.

Each of these examples resulted in a destiny-changing upgrade as a direct result of their surrender and sacrifice. David became the greatest king in Israel's history. Paul became the greatest of the apostles and wrote one-third of the new testament. Joseph was the greatest patriarch after Abraham and ruled over the known world of his day. Abraham laid his son on the altar and received back a nation chosen by God to reflect His glory. This same altar birthed for Abraham as many offspring as the stars of the sky because he became the father of all who believe. Jesus laid his life down on a hill in Jerusalem and picked up a bride from every tribe, nation, and every tongue.

Constantly putting our lives on the altar always results in death and upgrade. We die to the good, and the best of God resurrects off the altar. It seems that the Father is a serious investor always looking for a higher return. Jesus has several parables about talents and returns on investment. The Father is looking for a return, and He is an excellent rewarder for anyone who provides him with it. The Chronicler tells us, " *For the eyes of the Lord move to and fro throughout the earth that He may strongly support those whose heart is completely His.* " —*2 Chronicles 16:9*

God is betting on you

Jesus makes special promises about great returns to those who are willing to sacrifice, in some cases as much as one hundred fold returns. In God's math, $100 becomes $10,000 when we lay it on the altar. God doesn't ask us to die because he is mad at us. Through surrender, He prunes away every unnecessary thing hindering His return and your inheritance. It's a matter of family business. When we willingly die, He receives an increase and so do we. As we die to coping strategies, it frees us to run without encumbrances to bring more kingdom return for our Father. This brings Him great joy that He willingly shares with us.

The pruning analogy of John 15, where the Father prunes the branches so that they can produce more fruit, reflects the Father's heart. Pruning is painful but yields the Father and us a greater harvest. We can run from this for years, but sooner or later, we have to decide to die in the pit and get out or live out our days in the pit. Death in the pit brings resurrection while self-preservation in the pit brings a lifetime of death. You are going to die either way, why not die willingly and shorten your time in the pit? The pit is a graveyard of lost destinies. It is also a womb of new life and resurrected destiny.

God is a heart surgeon

Circumcision cuts away dead flesh. Under the Old Covenant, you were cut off from the people if you were unwilling to undergo circumcision. Circumcision as a child is one thing, circumcision as an adult, without modern day anesthesia, becomes a whole other level of surrender. Circumcision leaves permanent change and is easily recognizable. The deadness of the flesh has been cut away, and there is a purity and purpose that someone carries when they have spent their long night of the soul in the pit. There are no shortcuts, no one can do it for you, and you cannot avoid it. You will leave the circumcised flesh of your heart behind in the pit, or you will stay in the pit, clinging to dead flesh, until you let Him do heart surgery.

It's the valley of the shadow of our death and deep connection with Jesus. It's a personal place where our raw, naked heart meets with God. It's the cry of David in Psalm 139, "Where can I go to escape your spirit?" It is the place where we get stripped of everything, all except the love of God, and our value and identity in Him.

The pit purifies theology

The pit is also the graveyard of impotent theology because theology gets severely tested in the pit. The same theology above ground doesn't work in the pit. When Job crawled out of his pit, he uttered a statement that reverberates throughout the airwaves of human history. He shifted from knowledge to revelation in the pit, and the words that flowed out of his heart dripped with anointing; "I have heard of you by the hearing of the ear, But now my eye sees You; Therefore I retract, And I repent in dust and ashes." It's the anthem of the pit. It's the song sung by everyone who thought they knew God because they had read or heard some things about Him. It's the very thing that Jesus confronted the Pharisees with when He said, *"You search the Scriptures because you think that in them you have eternal life, it is these that testify about me." —John 5:39*

The pit has a way of showing us that knowing about God is not even close to the same thing as knowing Him. Knowing Him requires the pain of discovering that we have a heart and that God wants to cut away anything that is preventing Him from touching it, loving it, and owning it. He prizes our heart above anything else on planet Earth. It's the treasure and the pearl of great price all in one blood-pumping, life-sustaining heart. It's the part of us that God won't stop pursuing until He wins all of it. To put it mildly, He is jealous for all our affection. He is Hosea married to a prostitute, who keeps pursuing and taking us back even after we have sold our affections to one lover after another, each one promising us a temporary reprieve from the pain of our lies *(Hos. 1)*.

God is not controlling

It's critical to know, while we are carving evidence of another day on the wall of our pit, that God is not controlling everything. The devil is a master at getting us, through misguided theology, to blame God for all his stealing, killing, and destroying activity. This issue has to get settled in the heart of anyone who hopes to resurrect out of the pit with freedom and a tender heart intact. To be truly free, we have to receive revelation that God is not involved in that initial wounding that brought about the core lie. I have repeatedly witnessed the life-giving freedom that comes to people who finally realize that God did not cause the event that allowed the core lie to come into their hearts. Too frequently this realization comes after they have spent years serving a life sentence in the prison of wrong theology. It exiting to be there the day they finally receive their pardon from King Jesus.

I avoided discussing theology for a long time in sessions because most people who function in inner healing/deliverance warn you to stay away from it as it opens the door to disagreement. This became a contradiction to me as the Holy Spirit would whisper the word "theology" in my heart during a session. Every time I worked through their theological errors, I would watch people get wrecked with the goodness of God and get set free. This happened so many times that I finally quit fighting it and actually started including it in my inner healing/deliverance training seminars. Then I began to watch people in our training seminars get wrecked with the goodness of God as they were set free from false concepts of a controlling God who forces them to love Him while their hearts couldn't really trust Him. I have repeatedly watched anger at God melt like butter in the presence of a love encounter with Jesus.

Sovereignty does not imply control

God is God and sovereign over all. He is in control without controlling everything. Of the three theologies that the Holy Spirit has me address in sessions, "God is in control," gets addressed the most often. It seems so hard for the human heart to fathom being ruler over all without having to control everything and everybody. Fear and control always go together and are the most common demonic spirits I deal with in sessions. Because of our natural propensity to want to be in control, we can't imagine God having all control and not exercising it. There is no doubt that God sovereignly acts in ways that on the surface seem to have nothing to do with the person's free will. But if you dig a little deeper, you will typically see that God is serious about protecting, and honoring our ability to choose. Our God-given ability to choose is precious to Him.

The belief that God is controlling everything always gets exposed by the side effects it produces. These side-effects are evident in the lives of those who have suffered abuse. There are typically strongholds holding their hearts' in captivity to a belief that God either caused or okayed their abuse. Sometimes, the Holy Spirit will have me address this theology before He takes them back to a memory that Jesus wants to heal. He does this so the person will be able to accept the Jesus that shows up in the memory. It sets them up for healing when they meet the Jesus who usually tells them He is sorry for what happened to them or that the abuse is not what He wanted for them.

This is a hard Jesus to accept if you believe that God is controlling everything. The Jesus that does not give His stamp of approval to the stealing, killing, and destroying of the enemy has shown up thousands of times to set captives free right in front of me. False Jesus, which I have also encountered in sessions, cannot set people free. False Jesus cannot radically change lives to experience a deep intimate connection with God. The false Jesus I have encountered, attached to people, was only taking them further into confusion and bondage, but not freedom.

Janie died to theology and came alive

The first time I experienced this I was praying with Janie. About 15 minutes into our session, I heard the Holy Spirit say to me, "Theology." Because I had knowledge from the Holy Spirit that she had been abused I knew which theology He was asking me to deal with. I asked her if she had ever heard that God was in control and she said, "Yes." I then asked if she had heard that everything comes through the hand of God and she said, "Yes." I asked her if we would still be friends if I messed that theology up for her. She looked at me as if to say, "Oh are you so foolish to disagree with that? You can't possibly believe that God is not in control." She seemed annoyed but intrigued with the audacity I had to challenge, what was in her mind, orthodox, and centuries proven theology.

I upped the stakes of my audacity and said, "You are actually on a fool's errand." She said, "What do you mean?" I said, "You are trying to love someone you don't trust." I said, "That is an impossible task." Your head will try to play that game and convince you that you can, but your heart is screaming the whole time; "No, you can't." She looked at me and said, "That is my struggle. I know I am supposed to love God, but in my heart I know I don't, in fact, if I'm honest, I actually hate Him for what He let happen to me." I said, "I know, and if that is who God truly is then we are all just playing a religious game because the only people who can love that God are the ones who have never had anything bad happen to them." I said, "Without trust, it is impossible to have love." I said, "You can have control, co-dependency, and a host of things you might try to call a relationship, but you can't call it love because God is not dysfunctional."

I ended up leading her through the discussion that follows, and she let go of the errors in her former belief. I then led her into an encounter with Jesus in the memory of her abuse, and she got radically set free from the abuse, even after over 40 years of counseling.

Jesus broke the bad theology off before He appeared to her in the vision where He wept over her and apologized to her for what happened to her. She was crying so hard she could hardly talk and said, "Is it actually possible that Jesus is apologizing for what happened to me, and He has tears in his eyes and is saying to me He is sad for what happened to me?" She has never been the same after that encounter. She would never have gotten set free had she kept clinging to a belief that God gave the approval to the enemy to molest her.

What sets you free is not debatable
I am not going to claim to solve for you the 1,700-year-old debate concerning the sovereignty of God and the free will of man in a couple of pages of a non-academic, non-theological book. I do, however, know that it's not a scriptural issue. Ample scriptures support both

points of view, which is part of the reason this debate has echoed through the halls of Christianity for almost two thousand years. People have shed blood over this debate.

The Bible reveals your heart

In fact, I can argue for both cases from Scripture. Because it is not a question of one side having more verses to throw at the argument than the other, it forces the debate into a character of God issue.

In fact, I believe that there is something very unique about the way the Bible is written. The whole of the Bible is written in such a way that it actually reveals what's in your heart. You will gravitate toward passages and theology that are consistent with what is going on in your heart. That's why a theologian like St. Augustine started his journey entirely convinced that miracles are no longer necessary or a part of God's normal interactions with His church. Then, he did a complete one-hundred-eighty degree turn at the end of his life and fully embraced that miracles are for today in the article "City of God." He read the same Bible at the beginning as he did the end. The only thing that changed was what was in his heart, and it shifted the way he saw God through the exact same scriptures.

If the sovereignty of God and the free will of man debate scratches your itch, there are libraries full of volumes on this topic that you can continue researching. I am only presenting here what I have seen shift hearts and set people free in sessions. What I am convinced of, through thousands of case studies, is that there are lofty things raised up against the knowledge of God that get people stuck in a theological pit even though they may have ample scripture and theologians to back up their view. My experience has shown that they are not going to get out of that trap until they die to knowing about God and resurrect with an intimate connection to God; a God who willingly died for them; a God who is a whole lot more interested in a surrendered, willing heart full of love than a heart He has controlled into rote obedience. A prison guard can make you obey him, but he cannot make you love him.

You have free will whether you want it or not

I explained to Janie the same thing I usually do in similar cases. It goes with the idea that God had a choice to make before He ever created angels or mankind as to whether to give them free will or not. He could see all of the evil that would transpire if He did, yet He chose to give His creatures free will anyway. This is of course, limited free will. We did not choose our parents, the day of our birth, the timing, or the country we were born in. But the day our feet hit the ground we started having a lot to do with the way our life turns out. We have a lot of groping and seeking to do.

"And He made from one man every nation of mankind to live on all the face of the earth, having determined their appointed times and the boundaries of their habitation, that they would seek God, if perhaps they might grope for Him and find Him, though He is not far from each one of us; for in Him we live and move and exist," —Acts 19:26-28

God saw it all in what the Bible calls foreknowledge and yet He was willing to risk all the evil in the world to get one creature to respond to Him in love from a free, uncontrolled heart

God is love, neither are controlling

Did you know there are some things God can't do? God cannot choose to love. He can't choose to love because He is love. He can't stop Himself. Love oozes out of every part of His being. His own description of love in 1 Corinthians 13 says that it is not controlling, (does not insist on its own way).

"Love is patient and kind; love does not envy or boast; it is not arrogant or rude. It does not insist on its own way; it is not irritable or resentful; it does not rejoice at wrongdoing, but rejoices with the truth. Love bears all things, believes all things, hopes all things, endures all things."— 1 Corinthians 13:4-7

God's own definition of love and therefore Himself, since He is love, is that He is not controlling! James says that God cannot be tempted by evil, and He does not tempt anyone.

If what a person means when they make the blanket statement "God is in control," is that they have surrendered control of their circumstances to God, then I shout hallelujah and amen in hearty agreement. The whole purpose of the pit is to get us to surrender not just our circumstances but our life. But that is not the same idea that is caught when someone who has been through abuse hears the blanket statements that, "God is in control," and "Everything comes through the hand of God." What they hear, with admittedly damaged spiritual filters, is that God either caused or gave the okay for their abuse. Most people's hearts can't make a distinction between "God is in control," and "God is controlling everything." If God is controlling everything, the pit would not even be necessary since the whole purpose of the pit is to get us to surrender control of our lives and hand it over to God!

God is not evil

If God is controlling everything or everything comes through the hand of God, then He is ultimately causing or putting His stamp of approval on all the evil in the world. If He is putting His okay on every evil act, then He is ultimately responsible for all evil. You might be able to perform the mental gymnastics required that allows you to say you believe two entirely contradictory things at the same time, but your heart is much more truth-telling than that and will never fall for it. Your emotions will be in rebellion to your intellect and you will either have to develop a stronghold of numbing the contradiction or give it up in the pit.

Many times a person will bring up the book of Job as the template for explaining how God is controlling everything. Another example has to do with Peter when Jesus said that Satan was asking permission to sift him like wheat. These two are the ultimate case studies to prove that Satan has to get God's approval to attack.

Job is not a template for all suffering

First of all, these two examples happened while both Job and Peter were spending their season in Pattern 5, in the pit dealing with pride as full-grown men. Pride is an issue that God never protects when it is found on any of His children. It is open season on our pride 24/7. He gives grace to the humble, but He resists the proud. They make an excellent explanation for Pattern 5 but a terrible rationalization for

Pattern 2. In other words, both examples are for a specific season, not a blanket template to explain all suffering. Job is a template for Pattern 5 and was never meant to be a template to explain all suffering. Job will never explain child abuse or any other evil. Job explains that in the pit, God will put limits on Satan. Job explains that in the pit, Romans 8:28 kicks into high gear.

Secondly, both of these examples were full grown men who were very far along in their walk with God and were called to the witness stand of human history. Satan can only be in one place at one time, he is not omnipresent like God. These were unique cases of God and Satan trying a court case in the courtroom of planet Earth. In neither of these examples was a 6-year-old child being sexually molested by an adult.

Pride died in Job's pit

No doubt, Job was an amazing man who stood out above all others in his day. But his coping strategy of pride got revealed chapter after chapter, day after day, the more time he logged in the pit with his critical, religious friends. He started out great, but the pressure of the pit revealed what was hidden deep in his heart, and pride floated to the top for God to skim off. God wanted to radically increase the blessing and favor on Job's life, but pride was preventing the increase God wished to give Job. If He gave Job the outpouring of blessing while he had it connected to his good behavior, it would have put him in further bondage to a spirit of performance. When it got cut away, a double portion of blessing poured into the space made available by the Divine surgery on his heart.

Job seemed to be relying on his good behavior to guarantee God's blessing and protection. On more than one occasion, he wanted to get in God's face about it until the Ancient of days showed up in chapter 37 and told him; "Gird up your loins like a man." Code words from God that meant, "I have let you and your friends talk about who you think I am for 34 chapters, now it's my turn to finish circumcising the pride from your heart with words that are going to cut." From the sound of the text, that heart surgery was performed without anesthesia. God cuts right to the heart of Job's pride and removes all in one statement. *"Will you really annul my judgment? Will you condemn Me that you may be justified?"* —*Job 40:8a*

We have already seen Job's amazing conclusion at the end of the book with his shovel of pride broken and his heart circumcised and tender. Job had the clarity to make the statement to God that, "I have heard by the hearing of the ear, But now my eye sees you." That revelation caused him to fall on his face, retract his prideful statements, and repent. It's the same revelation God is looking for each one of us to receive.

Pride died in Peter's pit

In the case of Peter, he and the other disciples had just gotten through arguing about who was the greatest when Jesus warned him that Satan was demanding to sift him like wheat. The reason Satan was demanding was because he had legal access through Peter's pride manifesting in his heart as an open door to the enemy. He then made the boastful statement that he would lay down his life for Jesus. The reason it is boastful is because of Jesus' response that Peter, instead of dying, would actually go on to deny Him. Peter wasn't ready to die for Jesus at all, and both Satan and Jesus knew it.

Satan walked right through the open door of pride and poked Peter's core lie with his evil finger and Peter transformed instantly into a coward. He found out that not only that he was unwilling to die for Jesus, but also that he actually claimed to not even know Him three

times. The cock mocked his pride by crowing three times, one for each denial. But Jesus sought out Peter and did inner healing with him on the beach after His resurrection. Peter responded with three humble declarations of love, and it healed his heart. That inner healing propelled Peter to an upper room, the effects of which spilled out onto the streets of Pentecost, which he led, as well as three thousand souls to Jesus.

Job and Peter are two specific cases of Satan himself being involved at a critical time in a person's life of extreme destiny, in the Kingdom who was dealing with pride. These are such extreme cases that they make very poor templates to be used to explain all the evil that comes our way. The idea that Satan can only go so far because He has to get every evil act approved with God doesn't square with the God I watch every day weep over abuse. God giving permission to steal, kill and destroy does not provide me with comfort; it has the opposite effect on me and everyone else I have ever met that has been abused. It begs an answer to the question; What kind of father would open the front door of his house and allow a grown man in to molest his child? All of the theological dance steps in the world can't reconcile that thinking with a God you can actually trust.

Jesus hates child abuse

Can you imagine Jesus, when He walked this earth, coming upon a little 6-year-old girl being molested by a 20-year-old man and saying, "For the greater good, I'm going to allow this? She will grow up, write a book, and have a ministry that will help a lot of people, so for the greater good, I am going to go ahead and let this happen." Can you imagine Jesus saying that? I can't either. Here's what Jesus actually said about it. *"It would be better for him if a millstone were hung around his neck and he were thrown into the sea, than that he would cause one of these little ones to stumble."* — *Luke 17:2*

The millstone idiom used in this passage is Jewish, and it means that it's better that they were never born. There are levels of hell, and apparently, child abuse is at the bottom of that pit. In other words, if this abuser doesn't repent in his lifetime, it is better that he was never born. That doesn't sound like Jesus is allowing or okay with abuse.

"The thief comes only to steal and kill and destroy; I came that they may have life, and have it abundantly." — *John 10:10*

Thieves don't get permission

A thief, a murderer, or a destroyer does not politely ask permission before stealing, killing, or destroying. Have you ever had a thief politely knock on your front door and ask, "Hey can I steal your TV? And by the way, I am going to come back tomorrow and take the rest of your stuff and molest your family. Are you okay with me doing that?" No! Thieves don't ask permission. There is a reason Jesus called him a thief, it's because if he asks permission he is no longer a thief. And by the way, Jesus said, "I only do what I see the Father doing." Scripture declares that Jesus is the exact representation of the Father.

"And He is the radiance of His glory and the exact representation of His nature, and upholds all things by the word of His power. When He had made purification of sins, He sat down at the right hand of the Majesty on high." — *Hebrews 1:3*

Jesus looks like the Father

If we have a theology about the Father that we don't see in Jesus, we have to let go of that theology. We have to come to a place where we see that God really is good, infinitely good. Just like Jesus! He's not a contorted good, seen through the mental gymnastics of contradictory theology. He is just plain and simply, amazingly good! He is the prodigal Father, waiting to pour out His love on us and wash away the filth once we get sick enough of feeding pigs in the pit to return home.

Clearly, Jesus is not okay or giving approval for the attacks of the enemy that bring about core lies into our lives. These lies attempt to thwart the prophetic truth the Lord speaks over each of us in the womb. We have to see the clear distinction between the fact that Satan isn't getting permission for the attacks that serve to plant core lies in our hearts in Pattern 2, and the fact that God allows pressure in Pattern 5 in the pit to break us of coping strategies. Without that clear distinction, we will never be able to truly trust Him and therefore love Him. Confused thinking about the trustworthiness of God will place a ball and chain on the leg of our freedom.

Now that I have shocked your theology a bit, I want to word it this way, – God is in control, but love limits what He controls. I would also say that we have "limited free will." We have a lot of choices that affect everything from the quality of our daily life to our eternal estate. I would also say that God never acts in predictable ways but seems to allow us to see patterns.

Don't blame God in the pit

There is admittedly some mystery here but the thing we need to catch from this pattern is that God is sovereign above every circumstance, devil, and disaster. Yet He is calling each of us into a faith journey of fully surrendering to His Lordship. Only then does He have control of the surrendered parts of our lives and the power struggle between our will and His can end. This will allow us to surrender our lives in the pit and come out of it an empowered resurrected warrior preoccupied with Jesus and His kingdom instead of ourselves. We will discover in Pattern 5, that undeserved suffering releases undeserved gifts.

Who God is to us in Pattern 5: Yahweh = I Am

Yahweh is the answer God declared to Moses when he asked who shall I say sent me *(Ex. 3:15)*? "I Am," was a profound statement. He was declaring that He stands alone as the all-sufficient One, the One with no beginning or end, utterly independent, the One that does what He pleases, the absolute standard of truth, justice, love, and goodness, and the One that every other thing in the universe has its origin in and is subject to. I Am is the One we have to receive revelation of and come into intimate relationship with in the pit.

We have to see He alone reigns supreme over life and circumstances before we will ever surrender to Him. We have to see He is the very definition of good because things don't look good in the pit. When we finally see the great I Am, we will finally trust Him enough to give up control of our lives and die in His arms. The fruit that results from the pit is ridiculous. It's the kind of fruit the Israeli spies saw when they spied on the Promised Land and carried back grape clusters so large it took two men to carry one cluster suspended on poles.

The pit produces the new wine of the Kingdom, but it also fashions new wineskins to carry it in. The pit will be the single most painful season of your life and, at the same time, the most freeing. One look from Yahweh in the pit and the pit won't matter anymore because you will be free from the pit long before you ever crawl up out of it.

You will invest the rest of your life for another glance from the One with fire in His eyes, who invented love and who owns every answer to every question that you don't even know to ask. After you resurrect from your soul-sculpting season of the pit, you will have developed Job's clarity enough to echo his words. "Now my eye sees You."

Scripture: "Come, let us return to the LORD. For He has torn us, but He will heal us; He has wounded us, but He will bandage us". —*Hosea 6:1*

Tool: Shovel breaker

Activation:

- Ask God to meet you in the pit of your circumstances.
- Ask Him to show you what have you done to help create your current circumstances.
- Ask Him to show you what the enemy has done to help create your current circumstances.
- Ask Him to show you what pressure He is applying to get your attention in your current circumstances.
- Ask Him what you need to die to.
- Write down whatever He tells you during this time. Repent and surrender whatever He shows you and command any spiritual attachments to leave in Jesus name.

JOSEPH PRAYER

Pattern 6:

Death brings life

We surrender the pain-avoiding strongholds and exchange them for life.

Joseph's Pattern 6: Joseph died at the bottom of the pit of his prison cell, and the first green shoots of resurrected life broke through that well tilled soil. The evidence that confirms Joseph had died to self was the fact that Pharaoh had a God dream and the cupbearer remembered Joseph. God was now ready to bring the resurrected Joseph out of the pit. Nothing sends the fire and backing of heaven like sacrifice. God used the lows of the pit like a trampoline to propel Joseph onto the world stage. He started the process by giving Pharaoh a prophetic dream about the future of the world and the coming famine. He then turned the cupbearer's brain back on, and he remembered Joseph's name. Joseph was let out of jail to interpret the dream and step into the position and destiny God had for him. The shift in his attitude was evident after Pharaoh said to Joseph that he could interpret his dream. Joseph said in response; "It is not in me; God will give Pharaoh a favorable answer."

"Then Pharaoh sent and called for Joseph, and they hurriedly brought him out of the dungeon; and when he had shaved himself and changed his clothes, he came to Pharaoh. Pharaoh said to Joseph, 'I have had a dream, but no one can interpret it; and I have heard it said about you, that when you hear a dream, you can interpret it.' Joseph then answered Pharaoh, saying, 'It is not in me; God will give Pharaoh a favorable answer.'" — Genesis 41:14-16

Joseph's death to self: He came out of the two years of prison honoring God for his gifts. There was no self-promotion or deal cutting left in the language of his interaction with Pharaoh.

Joseph's promotion: God promoted Joseph from criminal to world ruler all in one dream interpretation. God used the gifts and calls that the enemy had attacked, as the very stick Joseph beat the enemy with.

You are guaranteed to get vertigo in this pattern. The upside-down nature of the Kingdom of God will become evident as you actually have to die in order to come alive. New, abundant, supernatural life gets released here like nowhere else, but it's going to cost you everything. It's the single most painful pattern of your life and at the same time the most freeing. The death we are talking about isn't physical, although sometimes it feels like it. I'm talking about when the compromises, excuses, games, lies, coping and pain-avoidance are finally over. You're dead and done, and it's the best place you could possibly get to because it's not only the place of surrender but, more importantly, it's the place of your resurrection. You get real, and finally see yourself and Jesus in the light of true identity. We have to arrive at this place to realize our part in our own story: No more rationalizing, running or coping, just raw honesty before the Lord and those who He has placed in your life. You've come home to your own heart by listening to the heart of Jesus. You are hemmed in by Him, and the lies and coping strategies are no longer a possibility. Growth, blessing, and gifting can now accelerate. The stone of your fleshly grave gets rolled back, and you walk out resurrected and fully alive.

Dead wait

You die here to the part of you that you have been dragging around like a ball and chain for years, because now God finally has His foot on it. You're not getting out of this pattern until you let Him cut that ball and chain off your leg so you can run forward into your destiny with real freedom, power, and gifting.

"Therefore, since we have so great a cloud of witnesses surrounding us, let us also lay aside every encumbrance and the sin which so easily entangles us, and let us run with endurance the race that is set before us, fixing our eyes on Jesus, the author, and perfecter of faith."—Hebrews 12:1-2b

The encumbrances, in the above passage, are the core lies and generational iniquities, that you've been dragging around for years. The sin, which so easily entangles us, describes the pain-avoiding strongholds developed through years of dealing with the pain of dragging a chain with a cast iron ball attached. You'll have to surrender both to get out of this pattern.

Running doesn't make it go away

Most of us run from this pattern our whole lives because we won't admit we even have a ball and chain on our ankle yet everyone else can see it. The pressures of the pit force us to kneel before the altar. We have to become so miserable in our "wilderness" that we give up and cry out to God in full surrender. We get brought to the point where we just don't have anything left in us to circle that mountain one more time. Contradictions have to get settled here. In this place, we learn to die and truly live at the same time.

Of course, another option awaits you in the pit, just in case you think you want a way out of surrender. You can stay in the pit and keep digging with your coping-shovel expecting a different result, but we all know what word that is defining. A large number of us will never lay our shovels down and get out of the pit. Scripture confirms this in the Exodus story. The Promised Land represented each persons' God-ordained destiny. Only Caleb and Joshua made it into their full destinies out of that first generation of millions. That number represents sobering odds for all of us to consider as we decide to cross the Jordan Rivers of our lives and leave the wilderness and the manna behind.

Manna doesn't taste like milk and honey

By the way, you were never meant to live on manna anyway. You were meant to live on milk and honey. Manna had little taste. It was the bare bones provision of a loving God. Even its name means "what is it?" He will always provide manna for you in the wilderness of your stronghold. But He never wants you to develop a taste for it.

He wants you craving the milk and honey of His best. He wants you hungering and thirsting for the specific destiny and flavor of milk and honey He crafted for you in your mother's womb. He promises that if you hunger and thirst for His righteousness, you will be filled. His righteousness carries you into the land just beyond the Jordan where the grape clusters are so big it takes two men to carry one of them on poles. Over there the milk and honey flow in an endless supply but you have to fight the giants in your land to get it. Giants cause most people to settle for manna.

Giant strongholds

Seven of the giants Israel faced when they crossed the Jordan represent some of the strongholds, and the spirits attached to them, that we will face if we choose to fully occupy our land. These giants and their demonic armies will have to die for us to fully live and occupy the land of our inheritance.

- *Jebusite* means to tread down or trample and represents the strongholds of shame, guilt, condemnation, heaviness, depression, self-hatred, self-harm, suicide, hopelessness, rejection, and isolation.

- **Girgashite** means the dwellers of the clay, or black mud and represents the strongholds of compromise, shutdown, dread, blocking, numbing, being stuck, doubt, unbelief, and skepticism.
- **Canaanite** means to compromise for wealth and materialism and represents the strongholds of mammon, greed, compromise, materialism, cheating, theft, jealousy, and comparison.
- **Hititte** means fear or no strength and represents the strongholds of fear, anxiety, control, people pleasing, isolation, false burdens, and terror.
- **Perizzite** means unwalled and unprotected and represents the strongholds of sexual immorality, lust, pornography, perversion, drug and alcohol abuse, addiction, eating disorders, and abuse.
- **Amorite** means the talkers and represents the strongholds of pride, boasting, bitterness, rebellion, witchcraft, manipulation, gossip, slander, comparison, control, strife, religion, and striving.
- **Hivite** means villagers, or dweller in a life-giving place and represents the strongholds of self-exaltation, deception, self-seeking, narcissism, and seekers of pleasure.

It's all yours

God speaks to us in the same voice that He spoke to Joshua before He crossed the Jordan and entered the land. He told him to be strong and courageous, and His voice speaks to us today: "I have given you the whole land; your enemies are already defeated at the cross, but you have to walk it out, and every place your spiritual foot treads will be yours." In other words, I promise you victory in every place you are willing to show up and face the giants in your land. But every place you are unwilling to face, will be a place of conflict and bondage for you, your generational lines, and those you lead.

Did you know that most of what God asks us to die to He has actually already killed? In Joshua's case, God had already defeated the giants in the land. Joshua just had to show up and claim it. We just haven't recognized that most of the parts of us that needed to die are already dead. God never asks us to die to our personalities. Even a brief look at creation recognizes that the amazing God we serve loves variety and incredible diversity.

You're different

The camel and the octopus both came from the same creative hand. He loves variety. How crazy would it be to have a world full of camels in the animal kingdom with no other animals? How crazy would it be for a camel to want to be an octopus? Dying to self doesn't create robotic, obedient Christians, gutted of any personal uniqueness. Yet the Jesus we have in our heads rarely matches the real Jesus. The real Jesus had his own unique personality and gifting. He had a sense of humor, emotion, and tears. He was real. And He had life without you, but He didn't like it, so He made you. Nobody like you has ever existed or ever will again. You are as unique to God spiritually as your physical DNA or your fingerprint.

The only person who wants homogenized Christianity is the devil. That is why cults all look, act, talk, and function the same. Everything alive inside of us rebels at even the thought of being devalued into a vanilla personality. The good news is that the more you die to what God wants you to die to, the more you become a more fully alive and colorful you.

You can't kill you

God asks us to consider ourselves dead to our sinful, pain-avoiding strategies. He's not trying to kill off parts of us He doesn't like. Mostly what needs to die is already dead *(Rom. 6:6-7)*. We just have to come into agreement with what He says died, which is sin. When we die to our own strategies for doing life apart from Him and lay our gifts and destiny on the altar (our Isaac), we get to come out of the wilderness: out of eating manna and into the milk and honey we have been looking for our whole lives. We had just mistaken it for the lingering taste of leeks and garlic left over in our mouths from our past.

God's lost and found

Jesus tells us that he who loses his life will find it and he who saves his life will lose it. The truth is that we can't kill what needs to die. We are told to consider it already dead *(Rom. 6:11)*. We have to crawl upon the altar and let the fire of heaven consume the sacrifice. Those that walk in power and the fire of God do so for one reason only: they have crawled up on the altar of God and died at some point in their life.

You're already dead

The main part of us that needed to die (our sin nature) was actually crucified with Jesus. That is made abundantly clear in Romans 6. Living out of this reality only happens with a few of us because the rest of us don't really believe that it is true. We have to consider what Paul said, that he who has died is free from sin, therefore, consider yourself dead to sin. Most of us don't consider ourselves dead to sin. He doesn't say kill off the sin in your life. He is telling us to recognize that this reality has already taken place, and we have to live out of this reality, if we want to be free. I don't have to sin anymore, because the source of sin has been killed by Jesus.

As we start to realize that we are actually dead to sin and therefore free from it, a couple of possibilities will begin to happen. First, we might think the task we are facing is too intimidating because the pain is too real. We don't think we can give up the sin that we have used to cope with pain our whole lives. Second, we can determine that, even though we feel like we're dying, the pain-avoiding strongholds are no longer options. They are recognized as the sinful ways we have become stuck in a pit. We can choose to face our pain and let Jesus heal it. Jesus wants to heal and radically transform us into His likeness, but it requires our agreement.

You're not who you were

Unfortunately, a large part of Christianity has been taught that we have a sinful nature, and the first time we hear someone say that we don't, after we're saved, sounds like heresy. Before you throw this book away as heretical, at least give me a chance to walk you through this Biblical concept. A lot more happened at your salvation than you getting a free-pass to heaven one day when you die. You have been radically changed. You are a new creation whether you realize it or not. Your whole nature changed when Jesus walked out of His tomb and into your heart.

It's true that we are born with a corrupted nature that has passed down through our ancestors (called our old man by Paul in Romans 6). Adam's corrupted nature has inhabited the souls of everyone born after him since the fall, with the only exception being, of course, Jesus, who was born of a virgin. Because we are all born separated from God through Adam's sin, which is passed down to us through our earthly fathers, many believe that we have a sinful nature until the day we die. They believe that this sin nature stays intact even when we believe in Jesus. This offers an explanation of our choice to stay in patterns of sin instead of being set free in Jesus. But it is evident in Scripture that we have been made entirely new in Jesus, including our nature which has undergone a radical change from sinful to righteous, from death to life.

The concept of the sinful nature was popularized by the NIV translation of the Bible. It is the only major translation that singled out six passages and translated the Greek word "sarx" as sin nature or sinful nature. The other major translations translated those same six passages as flesh, which is the proper translation for sarx. In fact, the NIV translated all the other occurrences of sarx in the original manuscripts as flesh. Flesh and sin nature are not even close to meaning the same thing (Col. 2:11, Rom. 7:25, Gal. 5:24, Rom. 13:14, Rom. 7:5, and 1 Cor. 5:5).

Given these issues, Zondervan announced an important change to the 2011 version of the NIV Bible. On page 8 of its Notes from the Committee on Bible Translation, it says, "Most occurrences of 'sinful nature' have become 'flesh.'" In other words, the NIV translators have recognized their error and have decided to use the same English word, "Flesh," for all occurrences of sarx in the same way the King James Version and nearly every other English Bible translates sarx. This is a good change, and it's already in effect.

Sin nature or free from sin

But the damage has been done, and a large portion of evangelical Christianity believes that they still have a sin nature even after they are saved. This contradicts clear verses in the Bible. The clearest is found in Romans 6.

"Knowing this, that our old self was crucified with Him, in order that our body of sin might be done away with, so that we would no longer be slaves to sin; for he who has died is freed from sin." — Romans 6:6-7

"For by these He has granted to us His precious and magnificent promises, so that by them you may become partakers of the divine nature, having escaped the corruption that is in the world by lust." — 2 Peter 1:4

"And in Him you were also circumcised with a circumcision made without hands, in the removal of the body of the flesh by the circumcision of Christ." — Colossians 2:11

"Therefore if anyone is in Christ, he is a new creature; the old things passed away; behold, new things have come." — 2 Corinthians 5:17

Even Ezekiel saw the nature change that was to come under the new covenant and prophesied about it in the book of Ezekiel. Our spirit has been made completely new; nature and all. In fact, we are an entirely new creation. Romans 6 says that we have actually died to sin. The question always arises: "Then why do we still sin?" I ask the question back; "Did Eve need a sin nature to sin?" The obvious answer is no. She chose to sin before sin had ever entered her world.

She sinned not because of her nature but because of deception and her own choice. All a believer in Jesus needs to sin is the same thing Eve needed: deception.

"But I am afraid that, as the serpent deceived Eve by his craftiness, your minds will be led astray from the simplicity and purity of devotion to Christ." — *2 Corinthians 11:3*

You act like what you believe

So why does all of this matter? Simple, if you believe you still have a sin nature, you have a baked-in excuse to live in sin patterns the rest of your life. You will live a life in harmony with the beliefs you have about your nature and who you are. I have seen people come completely out of a sin pattern by realizing that they no longer had a sin nature.

This is not irrelevant psychobabble. You will live consistent with how you see yourself. You cannot live differently than the belief you hold about yourself in your heart. The business world has a phrase they use called an "upper limit problem." It has been discovered that if you try to promote someone above the level they see themselves, they will self-sabotage. They will unconsciously do something to fail at the level above how they see themselves. If even the business world recognizes this reality, how much truer does it becomes in the spiritual realm? It matters how you see yourself. Remember, when your heart comes into alignment with truth, freedom happens. When you come into agreement with lies, bondage happens.

What do people do who have a sin nature? They live in sin. What do people who have a righteous nature do? They live a righteous life. When an unbeliever sins, he acts according to his nature. When a believer sins, he acts contrary to his nature.

Old man or new heart

Many will go to Romans 7 to prove they have a sinful nature. They quote Paul in the following passages and claim it as the normal Christian life. The problem with reading Romans 7 out of context is that doing so causes it to totally contradict Paul's clear theology and writing in the rest of the New Testament. It especially contradicts the previous chapter of Romans 6 that dogmatically declares that we are dead to sin. Not on life support; but dead.

"For I know that nothing good dwells in me, that is, in my flesh; for the willing is present in me, but the doing of the good is not. For the good that I want, I do not do, but I practice the very evil that I do not want. But if I am doing the very thing I do not want, I am no longer the one doing it, but sin which dwells in me."
— *Romans 7: 18-20*

Paul just stated in Romans 6 that you are dead to sin, and the very source of your sin was crucified with Jesus. He declares, because of this reality, that you are free from sin. There's a real problem with Paul stating that sin dwells inside of you *(chap. 7 vs. 20)* and at the same time saying your old man is dead, and that you are free from sin *(chap. 6 vs. 6)*. That sounds a bit schizophrenic to me.

Maybe the answer gets resolved if we realize that we are pulling Romans 7:14-25 out of context. In context, Paul seems to be conveying an entirely different concept. One that is consistent with the good news of the gospel found throughout the New Testament. One that gives us hope that Jesus has actually saved us from this body of death. One that says there is an answer to the strongholds in our life. This idea creates the potential for real freedom, and not just a theological explanation of why we sin.

Out of context and out of bounds

Pulling verses 14-25 out of context also means we have skipped the first half of the chapter. Reading in context is the only way to understand Paul's thoughts and the only way to really understand these verses. The first half of chapter 7 is all about an analogy of marriage to Jesus. It's a picture of what happens when we receive Jesus. It's also a picture of having a previous marriage before we met Jesus. The first husband, the law, has to die so we can legally marry the new husband, Jesus.

He spends the first several verses referring to the law as our first husband and describing the law and our interaction with it. The reason we have to die to the first husband, and him to us, is that the law is actually supposed to lead us to our second husband, Jesus. The law can never be the solution to sin. The law can only point out that you have a sin problem but cannot cure sin. The law leads us to the cure, our husband, Jesus. Once I am married to Jesus, I have to leave the law in the grave because it has served its purpose. That is the whole point of the first 13 verses.

In fact, Paul states in 1 Corinthians 15 that the power of sin is in the law. That's an amazing statement, which is expressed in another way in Romans 7. He says that he would not have come to know sin except through the law and that he would not have come to know about coveting unless the law told him not to covet. Then he says that sin took opportunity through the commandment and produced covetousness of every kind. Apart from the law, sin is dead. He makes this statement, which clears up why we have to die to the law and the law to us. I was alive apart from the law, but when the law came, sin became alive, and I died. He was alive apart from the law as a little boy, and when he became a Pharisee, sin came alive, and he became dead inside.

The law condemns, not cures

An analogy to what Paul is saying can be seen by comparing the law to an x-ray and sin to cancer. If a doctor suspects cancer in one of his patients, he will send them to get an x-ray. It will reveal what is happening on the inside of the patient, which may not be evident from the outside. The law does precisely the same thing. It points out the inside cause of all the problems, which is mainly our sinful nature. Once cancer gets identified, how crazy would it be to keep going back getting x-rays trying to be cured of cancer? In fact, getting x-rays over and over will actually cause cancer to grow. The law causes the same thing to happen when sin reacts to the commandment and sin actually increases as a result.

Many act this out as a result of seeing Romans 7 as an explanation of sin. We keep living as if we are condemned and under the law. But the purpose of the law is to point out that we have a sin problem. We have a sin nature on the inside of us that is producing sin, especially under the power of the law. The law should point us to Jesus as the cure. That's why Paul says the Law is our tutor that leads us to Jesus.

We go to Him, and He pays for sin and kills the source of sin inside of us so that we can be free of sin and alive to Him. We have the cure; we don't need to keep going back to get diagnosed over and over again. That activity will cause us to live under condemnation and become sin-focused even though our original source of sin is dead. This is why Paul says that the law had to die so that we could marry Jesus. You can't be married to Jesus and the law at the same time. They have diametrically opposing ministries. One points out sin and condemns you to force you to deal with it. The other eradicates sin and the source as it empowers you to live righteously by giving you a righteous nature.

The first husband has to die
Once you understand this marriage analogy and why we can't be married to the law and Jesus at the same time, you will understand what Paul reveals to us in verses 14-25. It's a picture of what it was like to be married to the first husband. Paul is the most explicit teacher in the Bible on the topics of grace, freedom from sin, and no longer being under the law. He didn't lapse for a moment with verses 14-

25 and use them as a description of the normal Christian life. He is showing us the exact opposite. The contrast of being married to Jesus versus the law becomes evident. He is showing us just how miserable it is to be under the law and trying to be good in your own strength. He sums up the whole chapter with this verse.

"Wretched man that I am! Who will set me free from the body of this death? Thanks be to God through Jesus Christ our Lord!"— Romans 7:24-25

Jesus saved us from being wretched and trapped in a body of death (our sinful nature) by crucifying it with Himself on the cross. He not only died for you, He died as you. He not only wiped out your sin debt, but He also did away with the very source of sin, your old Adamic nature.

After Paul describes what it was like being married to the first husband, the law, in the last part of chapter 7, He reaches the conclusion at the beginning of chapter 8. He says, therefore (after you understand chapters 6-7), there is no condemnation for those who are in Christ Jesus. He then gives you the solution in chapter 8.

"For the law of the Spirit of life in Christ Jesus has set you free from the law of sin and of death. For what the Law could not do, weak as it was through the flesh, God did: sending His own Son in the likeness of sinful flesh and as an offering for sin, He condemned sin in the flesh." — Romans 8:2-3

Living like a slave even when you're free

In other words, our sin nature is dead according to Romans 6, and we are not under or married to the law but to Jesus. We are therefore free from the bondage and domination of sin and free from condemnation even while we think we still have a sin nature. In other words, as believers in Jesus, we can believe we are not free from sin even though we are. In fact, we are not only free from sin; we are actually righteous, which means right standing with God.

With this mind-set, we will live like the slaves of Galveston, Texas who, on June 19, 1865, were finally informed of their freedom by the Emancipation Proclamation which was issued two years prior. For two years they lived as slaves even though they had been free for two years. Many Christians are living as slaves to a sin nature that is actually as dead as the law, giving people a right to own slaves. There was a war over setting those slaves free just like the war Jesus won at Calvary. He liberated you from the dominion of sin and the right of your oppressors to hold you in bondage. Are you going to live like a slave or grab the authority He bought for you and command your oppressors to leave and live like a free son or daughter of a king? Jesus paid a high price for you to live in freedom.

Nature or demon

What people have blamed on a sin nature is many times actually activity of the demonic realm. Sin functions on an uncontrollable scale not because of a sin nature but because of demonic attachments to wounds and lies promoting sin as a way to avoid the pain that manifests as a result of the devaluation of the soul. This genius plan gets us to grab sin as medication and then hands us an explanation through the idea of a sin nature. All the while demons take up residence in the wounds and lies they create. This occurs over a lifetime, and all the while we accept it as our nature. That thinking will never allow you to address the real issues in order to live in the real freedom that Jesus bought with His own blood. We are free from the corrupted nature of sin we inherited from our earthly parents and have been given a new nature by our heavenly parents. We now have authority over the demonic spirits attached to the strongholds they have created in us by managing the pain of believing their lies.

You're righteous, act like it

We are not just free from our sin nature, but we now have a righteous nature. Jesus doesn't just leave a vacuum in our spirits once sin has been dealt with. He filled the hole with righteousness; real righteousness, not just the make-believe type called positional righteousness. I am now righteous because of my new birth. I used to view this righteousness concept as wearing an old, dirty, moth-eaten coat that I wear on which Jesus sticks a pin of His righteousness. This is so that when the Father looks at me He doesn't see the old coat. All he can see is the bright, shiny righteous pin that Jesus hung on it. That's messed up! Jesus pulled the old coat off of me and burned it up! He then put a righteous robe on me, and that is now a picture of my new nature. I have had a complete nature change; I am not just wearing a pin symbolizing something that I don't yet possess. My spirit has been made righteous, it is so righteous that I am one spirit with Jesus. His Spirit is connected to my spirit. He cleansed it with His precious blood and deposited His very nature in my spirit. My soul (mind, emotions, and will) has not yet been redeemed yet but has to submit to my spirit. It has to agree that the righteousness that now dwells in me is who I have become. The Holy Spirit indwells my spirit and He can't dwell in something unclean.

If you weren't righteous you'd be dead

My spirit has become the equivalent of the Holy of Holies in the temple under the old covenant. If a High Priest tried to come into the Holy of Holies and his sins were not atoned for properly, he would die in the presence of the Shekinah—the glory of God—the Holy Spirit—that filled the Holy of Holies. Righteousness is serious business to God. He gave us a picture of what would one day take place in human hearts. The Holy Spirit, in your spirit, cannot dwell where sin does. You are not producing sin out of your spirit or nature, or you would drop dead just like the High Priest. Your spirit remains righteous even when your soul screws up and sins. Sinning is acting contrary to who you really are. You are a righteous son or daughter of the King. Your soul (mind, emotions, and will) has to be renewed with the truth that you have had a complete nature change so that your soul will start submitting and behaving that way.

You have the same power, which raised Jesus from the dead, in order to live righteously. You have the Holy Spirit dwelling in you and empowering your spirit, and giving back to you the righteousness you lost through Adam's sin in the Garden of Eden. When you put on the breastplate of righteousness, it signifies your soul coming into agreement with the righteousness that has already been birthed in your heart, which is what the breastplate protects. Your soul has to consciously agree with the Biblical truth that you have a new righteous heart courtesy of your new birth from your new heavenly parents.

"For by these, He has granted to us His precious and magnificent promises, so that by them you may become partakers of the divine nature, having escaped the corruption that is in the world by lust." — 2 Peter 1:4

This concept is clearly summarized in the following passage.

"Or do you not know that the unrighteous will not inherit the kingdom of God? Do not be deceived; neither fornicators, nor idolaters, nor adulterers, nor effeminate, nor homosexuals, nor thieves, nor the covetous, nor drunkards, nor revilers, nor swindlers, will inherit the kingdom of God. Such were some of you, but you were washed, but you were sanctified, but you were justified in the name of the Lord Jesus Christ and in the Spirit of our God."— 1 Corinthians 6:9-11

Paul is saying that the unrighteous cannot step into life in the kingdom and this list of sins is a small example of how their nature causes them to typically behave. He continues by saying these behaviors are a picture of how many of you lived before your nature change. He doesn't even say you are not involved in that activity anymore. In fact, the context of why He is saying this indicates they were still living like slaves to the nature that no longer belonged to them.

BUT changes everything

He says, BUT everything has changed. Don't you know that you have been washed, sanctified, and justified in Jesus? You don't have to live like this anymore. Your nature has totally changed because the Holy Spirit brooded and hovered over your spirit until your spirit was pregnant with the new birth that happened just like it did with Mary when she gave birth to Jesus. Guess what—Jesus' nature, free of sin has been birthed in your spirit. This is the concept Jesus used with Nicodemus when He told him, you have to be born again.

God is not cutting you some slack because you have a Jesus pin on your old, moth-eaten coat. He is calling you, son or daughter, "I have placed gold inside of you, a new nature, purpose, gifts, and destiny. "He is asking you the question, "Will you partner with me and mine the truth out of the rich deposits I already buried deep in your hearts and live like it? Will you allow me to transform you by renewing your mind with the truth of what has already been birthed in you?" If a revelation of righteousness ever gets settled in your heart, you will be dangerous in the kingdom, and you will start getting free of sin's dominion or stronghold over your life. You will use grace as an empowerment to live righteously instead of an excuse to be a slave to sin.

Truth frees freedom

I have a friend who broke a lifelong pornography addiction just by me showing him that his sin nature was dead. He explained the way he used to think by saying, "When lust would knock on the door, I would rationalize by saying; I have a sin nature; I am going to sin the rest of my life. This is my area where it manifests, and I am just prolonging the inevitable. I might as well go ahead and give in." He told me that after he learned that he was actually dead to sin, the next time lust knocked on the door, he said he thought, "Wait a minute, I am dead to sin, I don't have to obey this thought because it can't be mine since I am free from it. I don't have to open this door." The lifetime of pornography addiction broke, and he got free. It matters how we see ourselves.

He's knocking, answer the door

Jesus doesn't tolerate or explain away strongholds. He is pictured in Revelation 3:20 as standing at the door of our hearts and knocking for us to let Him in to have intense, supernatural communion with us. That passage is talking to believers trapped in their own pain-avoiding strongholds which have Jesus shut out of their hearts. What it doesn't say is that Jesus will enter through the door of our hearts uninvited. He is knocking because He will not come in uninvited.

"Behold, I stand at the door and knock; if anyone hears My voice and opens the door, I will come into him and will dine with him, and he with Me." — Revelation 3:20

In context, Jesus knocks on the heart door of either a church or individual who has become numb. It's represented by the lukewarm (numb) church in Laodicea. A numbed-out bride is not acceptable to the passionate King of Glory. He is fully alive and doesn't accept being unequally yoked to a bride that doesn't care and can't feel anymore and has settled for a life of retreat and compromise. He is reproving, disciplining, and trying to get this bride to lay her shovel of pain-avoidance down and crawl out of the pit of the core lie and let Him in. Look at verse 19, which comes right before He knocks.

"Those whom I love, I reprove and discipline; therefore be zealous and repent." —Revelation 3:19

Jesus' knock on the door of our hearts, parallels the ancient Jewish marriage tradition of the groom knocking on the door of the bride with the price of the bride in one hand and wine in the other. His bride is in need of the two most important things for all humans; love and belonging. Jesus has both in His hand as He knocks on the door of the heart of His bride.

The price He is willing to pay for her He actually has in His hands at the door. He is re-connecting her to her value which is the price love is willing to pay for her. Price settles the number one need for love or value. The wine He is holding represents the Spirit which reconnects her to her identity (belonging); she is one Spirit with Jesus. Her gifts, destiny, and very identity are directly connected to the new wine of the Holy Spirit. This settles the belonging or identity issue. He is basically standing at the door, holding everything she needs.

But she is chasing it illegitimately through other sources that are numbing her heart, and she is becoming dead in the process. If she will let Him in and get value and identity from Him, she will come alive and start living abundantly with Him, and the love affair that will ensue is enough to write an R rated romance novel over. That book is called Song of Solomon in the Bible, which is a picture of King Jesus pursuing His bride and her response to Him.

He wants you back

The passage in Revelation we have been looking at reveals that Jesus wants to awaken this bride to remember their wedding day. It's the renewing of their vows. Many couples do it after they have been married for years. He wants to reawaken the passions of His bride to come back to her first love. In verse 18 before the discipline or the knock, Jesus tells her to buy gold refined by fire to make her rich (reestablishing her value in Him), and white garments to clothe her shame (restoring her righteousness in Him) and eye salve to see (reestablishing her ability to see Him as her husband and herself as His bride). The bride doesn't see her real condition or know who she is anymore. Her pain-avoidance has blinded her eyes and choked the life out of her with all the soul-numbing activity. She is said to be wretched, miserable, poor, blind, and naked. She has become numb, she is lukewarm, cynical and unresponsive. Jesus won't leave her there. He loves her too much.

Jesus has been disciplining her so that she will become zealous and repent (passionately reconnected). He is knocking on the door of her heart through the pain of discipline (Pattern 5) to get her to feel again and recognize her condition. Words no longer work with someone who is deeply invested in their strongholds. It usually requires pain in direct proportion to the numb condition of the heart. The person in the Revelation passage has numbed out with money and all the soul-deadening activity that it can purchase. She has prostituted herself out to the world to minimize the pain of believing that she is not good enough and Jesus wants to reclaim her.

Pain seeks pleasure

What delays our surrender is the fact that pain seeks pleasure for relief. This gets extra confusing for those who have suffered sexual abuse as a child. At the same time devaluing pain is being inflicted, sexual arousal is occurring at an age where there is no ability to control or understand their bodies' response. Pain and pleasure get co-mingled, and sex gets disconnected from love. The shovel of sexual addiction gets handed to the abused the same day their devaluing core lie gets implanted in their hearts. I have seen Jesus heal this pattern of abuse and pain-avoidance so many times it's impossible for me to keep count.

Swap shoes

As we give up our running shoes of pain-avoidance and trade them in for the shoes of the gospel of peace, God will actually use our feet to crush the enemy. It is the ultimate payback for the same feet that have run their whole life from the pain of the enemy to be turned into the very feet that God places on the head of the snake to crush the life out of it, as Romans 16:20 declares.

Our partnership with God to defeat the enemy will require us to utilize the authority Jesus has given us to cast spirits out when we run across them. We don't want to ever hand the enemy more power and credit than they deserve. But burying our head in the sand and not utilizing the authority and command Jesus gave us to cast out spirits is like going to a nuclear war armed with a BB gun. There is a reason Jesus cast out spirits as much or more than any other supernatural expression of His Lordship. Demons can never become the focus of our walk, but they cannot be ignored, either. We have to fix our eyes on Jesus, the author, and perfecter of our faith, and if a demon gets in the way, we pull the trigger of authority and cast them out with power. Then, we go right back and fix our eyes on Jesus again.

Dead or alive

At the same time, I cannot cast my will out. There are things I cannot cast out that I have to die to if I want to fulfill my destiny and receive a full inheritance. I have to die to my desire to self-medicate with sinful behavior. I have to die to the selfish ambition that I think is going to be the cure to all my insecurities. I have to die to my right to be right. I have to die to the idols that the enemy has fashioned in my heart through pain and pleasure. I have to die to every approach to life that doesn't have Jesus sitting in the center of it. I have to die to my right to hold grudges and stay offended. I have to die to anger and vengeance. I have to die to stuffing problems and blocking memories thinking that they are healed because I can't remember them. I have to die to blaming everyone else for the way that I am responding to life. I have to die to guilt, shame, and condemnation. I have to die to every other road to the Father but Jesus. I have to die to my kingdom and surrender to His.

If I am willing to die to all that is not of Jesus, I will become more fully me than I have ever been. My true self and personality will be fully expressed for the first time in my life. My soul will be in submission to my spirit, and I will be free, truly free—not just free to do whatever I want, but free from bondage to anything. I won't be a slave to the opinions of others. I won't be a slave to false motivation. I won't be a slave to sinful desires. I won't be a slave to fear or control. I won't be a slave to low self-esteem or a devalued identity. I will actually realize that I have been made righteous and live that way.

I will become a blessing and will be truly blessed. I will know my purpose and will not let anything deter me from that purpose because nothing else will make me come alive. I will have tasted the real thing, and I won't be able to go back to the cheap substitutes. I will be like Jesus, and the enemy will find nothing in common with me. I will have become a calculated risk for him to attack because the Father will take every attack and turn it into a blessing for me. The Father will be beating the devil with his own stick on my behalf. I will have lost my life only to have truly found it. Jesus will be on His throne, and I will be seated with Him far above all rule and authority of the demonic realm, and they will be irrelevant to me.

The only way that I will be able to die is to know that Jesus is faithful and that He paid the ultimate price for me. He not only died for me, but He died as me, and whether I realize it or not I have already died with Him. The value or price He paid for me cannot be renegotiated. My value is a settled issue. Getting all my value from Him will allow me to recognize that I am dead to everything else.

In short, I will fully surrender to Jesus and die to anything else from which I get my value, and I will resurrect to live the abundant life that Jesus promised.

Who God is to us in Pattern 6: Jehovah-Jireh = The Lord Provides or Sees

This name only occurs once in the Bible *(Gen. 22:14)*. It's the name Abraham called the place on Mount Moriah where God provided the ram caught in the thicket as a substitutionary sacrifice in place of Isaac. It's the name describing the God who sees our need and then provides. The part of us that has to die is the part that wants to provide for ourselves. Jehovah-Jireh is who we need an intimate encounter with at our Mount Moriah in Pattern 6. It's in death to self that we become the most like Jesus: our substitutionary sacrifice, provided by Jehovah-Jireh. If we follow Jesus, He will lead us straight to Calvary where we will crawl right up on the cross with Him. Make no mistake, dying to self is an excruciating process.

We can neither make it happen nor determine the time or place it is required of us. We just have to stay willing to crawl up on our crosses the moment it is required of us. It is seldom a one-time death and resurrection. There is a reason we are told to pick up our cross daily. The one who provides will meet you on the blood-stained road that leads to Calvary's hill. He knows that road well, His head was down under the weight of the cross, and He probably studied every pebble along the way to the hill of His humiliation and victory. Even in death, He provides everything you need to live. He even provides the faith we need to resurrect out of our dead nature. It's the old wineskin that we shed so that we can put on the new wineskin that will hold the new wine of the Spirit waiting to fill us up. Dying seems to shift our desire from the provision to the provider. If I cling to the provision, I will need more tomorrow; If I cling to the provider, I won't need anything else.

Scripture: "*Behold, I stand at the door and knock; if anyone hears My voice and opens the door, I will come into him and will dine with him, and he with Me.*" —*Revelation 3:20*

Tool: Jesus is knocking

(Jesus is knocking on the doors of our hearts where we have shut Him out. This is the part of our heart that is either shut down or running to sin as a way of avoiding pain. We meet Jesus at every door of our heart that He wants to knock on to let Him in to fellowship and to remove the pain-avoiding strongholds).

Activation:

• Ask Jesus to show you a vision of which door of your heart He is knocking on. (One at a time, go to each door He knocks on in the following way)

- Ask Jesus to identify the door and the pain behind the door.
- Ask Jesus to invite the part of your heart that is guarding the pain of that door to come forward in the vision.
- Ask that part of your heart if he/she will allow Jesus to rebuke the upper-level spirit that has partnered with that part of the heart to guard the door of the room that contains the pain.
- If you get permission, say: "Jesus, I ask that you permanently remove the cosmic entity of _____, and I pray in agreement with you. The Lord rebuke you, the Lord who chose all of my heart rebukes you in Jesus' name."
- Ask Jesus to reconnect with that part of the heart with Him in the vision.
- Ask Jesus to release the trapped pain, emotion and trauma out of the compartment and ask Him to remove the door.
- Ask the Holy Spirit to completely fill that compartment with His presence and declare it as kingdom territory.
- Write down everything He shows you, so you will know how you are trying to cope with life apart from Jesus. Repent of every strategy and stronghold and surrender them to Jesus and ask Him to take away the desire to self-protect and self-medicate.

JOSEPH PRAYER

Pattern 7:

Jesus is the ultimate pain killer

God takes us back to our pain source to forgive those involved,
heal us, and set us free.

Joseph's Pattern 7: Joseph was sitting on the throne in Egypt, but a big part of his heart was still sitting in prison. God brought Joseph's brothers to Egypt to save the Hebrew people from famine and to set Joseph free. God needed to revisit, with Joseph, the memory of his brothers' betrayal in order to heal the wounds of his heart. God brought the memory right to Joseph's doorstep when his brothers showed up. His three chapter response when they reentered his life in Egypt displayed the unforgiveness, anger, and vengeance that was buried so deep in his heart that he couldn't get himself free. He finally kicked everyone out of the room except his brothers, and the inner healing began. He started weeping so loudly and openly in front of his brothers, the Egyptians could hear him outside the building. Joseph got real with them for the first time since they had reconnected in Egypt by telling them his true identity. He then forgave them. He was now free to walk out his God-spoken destiny without hindrance.

"Then Joseph could not control himself before all those who stood by him, and he cried, 'Have everyone go out from me.' So there was no man with him when Joseph

made himself known to his brothers. He wept so loudly that the Egyptians heard it, and the household of Pharaoh heard of it. Then Joseph said to his brothers, 'I am Joseph! Is my father still alive?' But his brothers could not answer him, for they were dismayed at his presence. Then Joseph said to his brothers, 'Please come closer to me.' And they came closer. And he said, 'I am your brother Joseph, whom you sold into Egypt. Now do not be grieved or angry with yourselves, because you sold me here, for God sent me before you to preserve life.'— Genesis 45:1-5

Joseph's Inner Healing: He wept and released all the pain and trauma of his brother's betrayal. He got real before them and forgave them, and it set him free to rule without pieces of his heart disengaged.

Sometimes, we can't move forward until we go backward, and Pattern 7 invites Jesus to answer and heal the hurts of the past. Frequently, the enemy will use something from our past to shut down our present. Lie-based pain and unforgiveness handcuff us to the enemy and keep us blocked from intimacy with God and those we care about. Every day is a jubilee year with Jesus. Every 50 years everyone in Israel would cancel all debts and set all slaves free. Because of Jesus' sacrifice and routing of our enemies, every day is a jubilee year on His calendar. Part of what He declared in Isaiah 61 when He went into the synagogue in Nazareth was, "To proclaim the favorable year of the Lord." We looked at this proclamation of Jesus in Pattern 4 but did not look at this part of His declaration.

"To proclaim the favorable year of the Lord."
—Luke 4:18-19

Go backward to move forward

The favorable year of the Lord was a year of favor, a Jubilee year. Jesus declared that day, "Today this Scripture has been fulfilled in your hearing." In other words, He was ushering in a Jubilee that would last from now on. This means every day is a day to be declared free. This motivated Him to also declare, "To proclaim release to the captives...To set free those who are oppressed." Being held captive to traumatic memories and oppressed by demonic tormentors because of unforgiveness doesn't have to be our lot as lovers of Jesus. Jesus has declared every day as a year of favor or Jubilee.

On occasion, I have someone ask me, isn't revisiting the past counterproductive to everything Jesus accomplished on the cross? Didn't Paul say, "But one thing I do: forgetting what lies behind and reaching forward to what lies ahead?" I assure you, God is not asking us to live as victims of our past. Jesus laid His life down for that not to happen. Yet He will take us back to the memories that the enemy uses like a chain on our neck to keep us bound over a lifetime in order to set us free. That initial source of pain has to be surrendered to Jesus for us to receive healing for our soul wounds and to expose the lies they cause us to believe as a result. This will usually free us to receive the freedom-producing truth of Jesus, which permanently cuts the chains from the past. These healing moments also give us the opportunity to forgive those involved. It frees us to walk out of the self-imposed prison of unforgiveness shared with the demonic cellmates that torment us there (Matt. 18:34).

In fact, Jesus actually takes us back to heal us just like He did Joseph who was not walking in freedom before this part of his story transpired. He was in a place of fighting the pain of betrayal from his brothers in his flesh before he finally surrendered it. That surrender not only set Joseph free but also resulted in saving, from starvation, the Hebrews at that time, which consisted of his immediate family. I have seen the effects of Jesus setting one person free, and as a result, whole families get set free, and I have seen it multiple times.

It set Joseph free

Joseph played games with his brothers for three chapters before he got to the point of releasing the pain and forgiving them. He was wrestling with unforgiveness, bitterness, judgment, and revenge. He wouldn't even tell them who he was. He falsely accused them of being spies, had Simeon bound and placed in jail while the others went home to let him see what that felt like. He placed his silver cup in their travel bags to have them arrested. He even put money back in their bags that they had brought to pay for the grain and it really messed with their heads. It's interesting to notice, in the story, that Joseph's antics caused the shame and guilt of his brothers, for what they had done to him, to come floating to the top even before they found out the person that was tormenting them was actually Joseph.

"Then they said to one another, 'Truly we are guilty concerning our brother because we saw the distress of his soul when he pleaded with us, yet we would not listen; therefore this distress has come upon us.' Reuben answered them, saying, 'Did I not tell you, 'Do not sin against the boy,' and you would not listen? Now comes the reckoning for his blood.' They did not know, however, that Joseph understood, for there was an interpreter between them. He turned away from them and wept."
—Genesis 42:21-24

Buried but not forgotten

All of the attitude and actions that manifested in these three chapters were already buried deep in Joseph's heart. They were locked away behind a door of his heart with a sign on it that said do not enter. God just knocked on that door with his brothers' appearance so that Joseph could be delivered and his brothers set free. He would have been an ineffective world leader with all of that sin stuffed in his heart. By God forcing Joseph to deal with the memory of his brothers and forgiving them, it became a Jubilee day for Joseph and his brothers. It set Joseph free and presented his brothers with the grace to get free from the guilt of their past as well. They also had a significant leadership role in shaping Israel. The 12 tribes of Israel came out of these brothers, including Joseph's two sons. Levi was the only brother not counted because from his line came the priestly line who's inheritance was the Lord.

Get real and get free

Joseph finally realized that all of his mistreatment of his brothers was not getting him set free. So the next trip the brothers made back to Egypt resulted in Joseph kicking everyone out of the room except his brothers and then the inner healing started. He finally surrendered his unforgiveness, bitterness, rejection, anger, and retaliation. He began weeping so loudly that the Egyptians could hear him outside the building, and even Pharaoh's court heard about it. He finally got real and said, "I'm your brother Joseph." Then he forgave them. He said, "Now, don't be angry with yourselves, because you sold me here, God sent me before you to preserve life." In an instant, Joseph found freedom! God can heal a lifetime of pain in a single moment of surrender. I watch Him do it on a daily basis.

God takes us back so that we can press on, as Paul says in the verse following the one I quoted at the beginning of this chapter.
"But one thing I do: forgetting what lies behind and reaching forward to what lies ahead, I press on toward the goal for the prize of the upward call of God in Christ Jesus." —Philippians 3.13b-14

We will not be able to press on until we get healed from the pain and lies of our past that hold us captive in space and time and forgive those involved. An argument about whether it is accurate or not to revisit our past to get healing won't set you free. But one encounter with Jesus will, when He shows up in a memory and redeems it, He heals your heart, replaces lies with the truth and sets you free. Once that memory gets healed, you can let the blood of Jesus seal that door shut once and for all.

Peggy's pain

Peggy is someone that I prayed with who experienced exactly what I am talking about. Early in our session, I saw a vision of her as a little 5-year-old girl with a pink dress on, and she was happy and spinning in a circle. Then all of a sudden the screen in my mind went black. I knew that something traumatic had happened. I told her my vision and asked if it meant anything to her. She said, "I have no memory of anything that happened, but at about that age I started refusing to wear a dress anymore, and I pulled all of my eyelashes out so that, 'He' wouldn't like me anymore." She said, "I don't even know who he was."

She had been in therapy for over 40 years, and everyone she counseled with had sensed that she had gone through a traumatic event but could never get her to remember it. She had even been through hypnotism to try and remember. Deep in our session I had her ask Jesus to show her where the painful emotion was being held captive, and He showed her a 1940s era car, but it looked new. I had a sense this was the place where the trauma had taken place in the vision I had seen earlier. I had her ask Jesus if it was safe to go back to that memory and He said, "No, not yet." I suggested to her that we take a break which we did for about 20 minutes. I then asked her if she wanted to give it another try and she said, "Yes."

She quickly went back to the car in her vision, and I had her ask Jesus if it was safe for Him to show her what had happened in the car. She started to weep uncontrollably. I sat there in silence for about 15 minutes, then she started to calm down, and when the weeping stopped, she opened her eyes and looked at me. I asked her if she wanted to share with me what had just happened. She told me that in the vision, Jesus had taken her, as the little girl, and sat her in his lap. He then pulled out still pictures and showed her just enough for her to see what had happened without it being graphic and re-traumatizing.

Her uncle had sexually molested her in the car when she was 5 years old, and she was wearing a pink dress. We dealt with the lies that came into her heart that day, and Jesus totally healed the heart of that 64-year-old woman who had been living with the side-effects of that trauma for almost 60 years.

She said that she had always had an irrational hatred for the color pink. She had even made herself buy things that were pink to try and get over it, but she would end up throwing them away. This memory was tormenting her and manifesting as different strongholds, even though she had no conscious memory of it. Jesus revisited the memory one time and healed it. The stronghold side-effects went completely away, and she will never have to go back to that memory again.

The past isn't behind you until Jesus heals it

I agree wholeheartedly that we cannot live in the past and that there are no rearview mirrors in Christianity. But the past has to be surrendered to Jesus before we can do that. Stuffing the past and quoting scripture will not get it healed. Let Jesus revisit it, heal it, and then we can quote scripture, and it will be effective because we won't be harboring bitterness and judgment, locked away in a jail cell with demonic torturers.

Healing the past is precisely what Jesus said that He came to do. He declares through Isaiah 61; "He sent me to bind up the brokenhearted." We have already seen that the Hebrew word translated as brokenhearted is "Shabar," and it means fractured. He is healing hearts that are in a million pieces. That is going to require a visit from Jesus to our past. The difference between Jesus visiting our past and us or anyone else trying to fix us is that He can heal memories with one visit, with one word, with one touch. We keep going back and getting stuck by playing the blame game and fantasizing about what life would be like if we had not gotten hurt. That kind of activity of revisiting memories is the Devil's playground. That is not what

Jesus does when He goes back to a memory that has someone trapped. He heals it so we can press on to all that God has for us.

It is the enemy that gets us to revisit our past in a way that becomes unhealthy and nonhealing. He takes many of us back on a daily basis to revisit the devaluing-lie and the pain of the past through emotional triggers and pain-avoiding strategies that have become uncontrollable reflexes to any threats he sends our way. He can reduce us to the emotional maturity of a 6-year-old just by a look, a word, a smell, an attitude or anything that feels a little too familiar when the right button is pushed on a memory that isn't healed.

At the same time, he will do everything in his power to prevent us from revisiting the memory with Jesus. He will even use Scriptural logic to keep us trapped. When we go back to the memory while holding hands with Jesus, the memory gets healed. The enemy wants us to keep Jesus as far away from our pain as possible because he knows that when Jesus puts his fingerprints on our pain it's over. The enemy can't use that memory anymore to trigger us back to a cosmic jail with imprisoned emotions and responses.

Speaking Portuguese in Scotland

A great example of this happened when I was on an inner healing/ deliverance trip with several others to Scotland. One night, there was a lady who a team member was praying with, and he asked if I would assist him. I came over, and he filled me in on the fact that she had been prayed with the previous year by the same team member and others on the team and they had some breakthrough, but something seemed to still have her blocked and in pain. As we prayed with her, we uncovered that she had experienced three miscarriages in her past and it had never come up before with the team. As I led her through prayer, she invited Jesus into her painful memory. All pain and trauma were released and all lies were exchanged for the truth. It was a powerful moment, but I had no idea how powerful until the next day.

While we were in the memories of those miscarriages, I had her hand each baby to Jesus in a vision. As she wept, I prayed in tongues over her. The next day she came up to my team member and told him what had happened, and he said, "You have to tell Ray." When she came over to me, I noticed her countenance was completely different from what it was the previous night, and she had a big beautiful smile on her face. She said, "I have to tell you something that happened last night when you were having me hand my babies to Jesus, and you were praying over me in tongues; You were speaking in perfect Portuguese." She said, "I lived in Brazil for 10 years, and I am telling you that you spoke perfect Portuguese to me. You were saying; 'Hand Him the cup, hand Him the cup, hand Him the cup.'" I was stunned and started to weep.

I instantly remembered Jesus' moment in the garden of Gethsemane when He asked the Father to take the cup from Him. The lady had been drinking the very painful cup of three miscarriages in silence for years without relief. Here I was, without knowing it, telling her three times to hand Jesus the cup, one for each baby. It was a cup that Jesus had already drank for her and those babies 2,000 years ago. The thought of that almost dropped me to my knees. Later I wondered if I had really spoken in Portuguese or did she have the gift of interpretation? I quickly came to the conclusion that I didn't care which it was, it was still a miracle either way! One moment of revisiting a devastating memory with Jesus and she was healed, and I was wrecked and more in love with Jesus.

Memories manifest until healed
The enemy knows that if he can convince us not to let Jesus into that painful part of our heart, he can keep us reliving the event every day of our lives. You can hold a beach ball of pain underwater for a while, but sooner or later it is going to pop out of the water in torrents of anger, sexual addiction, drug addiction isolation, self-harm, people-

pleasing, or whatever your pain-avoiding stronghold of choice is at that moment.

When we react to the unresolved memory and emotions, we think we have an anger issue or a people pleasing problem, (whatever is manifesting) and never understand that the source of it all is a wound and a lie from a memory. Letting Jesus into our painful past for a moment is not revisiting our past in a way that is antithetical to the way Paul is describing pressing on. He is telling us to not live in the past. He is not saying never go back to a painful memory and let Jesus heal it. Joseph's story completely contradicts that thinking.

Inner healing without inner healing

Sometimes, Jesus does inner healing without going through an inner healing session. God can heal our hearts anyway that He wants, and we don't have to be in a session to be radically healed of memories and soul wounds of the past.

One Sunday morning at church, worship was really going strong with everyone engaged, and my Pastor, Michael, called out a word of knowledge about people who were carrying pain from their past to stand up. My niece, Chelsea, was sitting next to me and she stood up. Michael asked us to lay hands on anyone around us who were standing, so I did. As I remained seated, I placed my right hand on her back and started to pray very lightly in tongues as we worshiped. She began weeping. I started feeling the presence of the Holy Spirit very strongly, and my tongues increased in volume. The music was loud enough that it drowned out my speaking in tongues. I heard the Holy Spirit tell me to grab her hand with my left hand and place it on her stomach with my hand on top of hers. I did what He said and kept praying in tongues very intensely. She was crying so hard that she could barely stand up.

I don't know what I'm doing

I knew something profound was happening and I knew I was a part of it but didn't have a clue what was happening. This all went on for about 10 or 15 minutes. She then sat down, and the service continued. I served on the altar team that day and did not get a chance to talk to her before she left. She had been through a tough season in her life that included two unwanted pregnancies, in which the babies were given up for adoption, drug addiction, as well as jail time. She had landed back on her feet, and her life was back on track, but she struggled with what she had done, especially with regard to her babies.

Immaculate reception

I called her when I got home and asked her what had happened. She told me that when I grabbed her hand and placed it on her stomach, with my hand on top of hers, she was suddenly in heaven and it wasn't a vision. She had a throne room encounter and became totally unaware of the church and myself. She was standing in the presence of Jesus; He was beside her, in the same position I was in, with His hands in the same position as mine. She said she realized His hands were on her womb as He thanked her for carrying his children and not aborting them. He honored her for carrying lives that He had prophesied destiny, gifting, and calls over while in her womb. I then knew why she had been crying so hard that she had to hang on to the chair in front of her to keep herself from hitting the floor. I knew because I was crying on the phone and I was unable to stand as she described that heavenly encounter. She was healed in an instant by Jesus of all the shame, guilt, and regret she had from her season of rebellion. The prodigal Father had just reconciled another one to Himself through Jesus.

We're body, soul, and spirit

Understanding the strategy of the enemy to wound our souls and bind us in chains to unhealed memories requires a little closer look at our makeup as human beings. The enemy has had millennia to study our make-up and develop strategies to steal, kill, and destroy anyone who would dare go against his kingdom of darkness. He knows full well that we are tripartite beings made up of body, soul, and spirit. *(Gen. 1:26-27, 1 Thes. 5:23, Heb. 4:12).* This understanding inspires as much or more hatred from the enemy for humanity than any other aspect of our being. Angels are never said to be made in the image of God: that attribute is reserved for humanity alone. We stand alone as the only image bearers of God in all of creation.

The body is the physical part of us that is not only seen but includes the intricate unseen parts including the organs and structures that make up our physical body and its function. The soul is made up of the mind, emotions, and will. The spirit is the receptacle and "meeting place" for the Holy Spirit after we are born again and other spirits before we are born again. The language of the Bible describes someone who hasn't come to faith in Jesus as being dead. This can create an idea that an unbeliever's spirit is inactive. That is not the case; death in this sense is describing separation. The unbelievers' spirit is separated from the life of God which is only found in Jesus. But their spirit is very much active otherwise there would be no occult activity or false religion among unbelievers.

The spirit leads not the soul

Our spirit was designed to lead, not the soul. Yet ever since the fall, this has been hijacked. Mankind is now led by the soul instead of the spirit until our new birth in Jesus. As a result of the new birth, the spirit is reawakened with the Holy Spirit and restored to holiness and righteousness and made blameless and alive before God *(1 Cor. 1:30, 2 Cor. 5:21, Heb. 10:10, 14-18).* The spirit in the new covenant believer is the equivalent of the Holy of Holies, the most sacred room in the temple, under the old covenant. *(Heb. 10:19-22)* This is the room or container of the Ark of the Covenant where the presence of God in the form of the Holy Spirit resides. That's why Paul tells us that our body is the temple of the Holy Spirit. And it proves that our spirit is now righteous.

Under the Old Covenant, the temple was where the presence of God dwelt. Right before Jesus was crucified, he told the religious Jews that he was leaving their house desolate. What He seemed to be saying was that the Holy Spirit (the presence of God) would no longer be found in the temple. He was moving into human hearts. That's why Paul tells us that our body is the temple of God. The Holy Spirit still dwells in the temple, except the location of the temple has changed. That location is now found in the hearts of followers of Jesus. When your soul submits to your spirit, by default, the Holy Spirit is leading, since He indwells our reborn human spirit. When someone met with God, through the High Priest, in the temple, they brought their soul into submission to the Holy Spirit or presence of God. Your soul submitted to your human spirit, and therefore, submitted to the Holy Spirit—

expresses the same act. And because your spirit has been made righteous by Jesus, when your soul submits to your spirit, you live righteously.

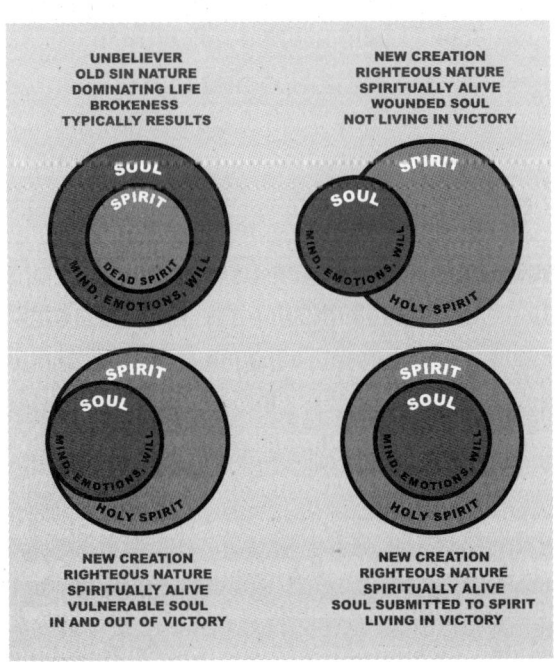

Soul control

The enemy knows that if he can cause the soul to be in control instead of the spirit, this will undermine the divine order and the destiny of the person involved. Demons wound the soul at such an early age so that the pain and devaluation cause the soul to seize control. This starts a lifetime of self-medicating or self-improvement strategies to fix itself or numb the pain which prevents the spirit from leading. This programming pattern of the soul began after the fall. Before the fall, the spirit of Adam and Eve led their souls. During and after the fall, their souls seized control through a combination of intellectualism, shame, guilt, fear, control, or whatever way the soul is trying to avoid or deal with the pain

of being devalued. In fact, the original temptation expressed this concept. As Satan convinced Adam and Eve to lead with their minds to pursue knowledge of good and evil apart from God, they became disconnected from their spirit. As a result, they suffered spiritual death or separation which ultimately resulted in physical death.

From the point of creation until the fall, Adam and Eve's spirits were in perfect communion and connection with God, and their souls (mind, emotions, and will) were in complete submission to their spirit. Satan knew that to win, he had to disrupt the divine order and engage the soul by waging war against the mind through reason and the temptation of power through knowledge. He knew he could not win against a righteous spirit dominated by the Holy Spirit.

Wounded souls require attention

Let's imagine God's plan for you is to walk five miles a day and engage the people you meet with the love of Jesus through your unique gifting. Right before you leave the house to go out for the first time, the enemy smashes your foot with a sledgehammer. What are you going to be thinking about while you are walking the five miles?

You are going to be thinking about how much your foot hurts and probably not that much about the people you are engaging, let alone doing it in the way God asks you to. You are going to be looking for a drug store to get something for the pain, probably a bandage to wrap the foot with and maybe some crutches. Every step becomes another distraction from your communion with God, your task at hand, and from expressing the love of God to the people you encounter.

That is a silly but memorable analogy for why the enemy wounds the soul. He wants you to spend all of your time thinking about the pain of your soul and how to pursue fixing yourself. He wants you consumed with getting relief instead of pursuing your destiny, gifts, and call. He even wants to get you seeking gifts as a way to relieve the devaluation of the soul. Soul pain makes us subjective and selfish because all pain seeks pleasure. Severe pain causes us to pursue intense levels of pleasure. The cruelty of religion becomes evident when it tells someone to stop the pleasure-seeking without offering to heal the pain. Religion is about sin management out of the flesh and not sin eradication through the healing and righteousness of the Spirit. Satan is the author of all false religion. Think about it, he wounds the soul, hands you the way to medicate the pain, then shames you through religion for medicating it. This creates even more desperation and more pain, and the cycle continues. It is a genius strategy to keep you trapped in a cycle of hopelessness and despair.

Soul vs. spirit

Paul discusses the difference between living out of the soul versus the spirit in the following passage.

"But the natural man does not receive the things of the Spirit of God, for they are foolishness to him; nor can he know them, because they are spiritually discerned."
—1 Corinthians 2:14

The word translated natural man is the Greek word Psuchikos. It means soulish, what is natural as it relates to physical life. (Helps lexicon 5591 psyxikós)

In context, this passage expresses the concept of fallen man with an unredeemed spirit being led through life by his soul, which is why I like the translation "soulish man" better than "natural man." This concept could just as easily describe a born-again believer in Jesus being led by his soul instead of his spirit, which is where he would receive the things of the Holy Spirit. God wants this order reversed which is why, at salvation, He totally redeems the human spirit and crucifies our old Adamic nature. We now have a righteous nature to live out of if we will surrender to that reality.

Mind game

Satan's overall strategy hasn't changed since the beginning even though his techniques have gotten progressively more evil through time. He wages war against the soul, typically through lies introduced to the mind in painful circumstances, to control the person's body, soul, and spirit. He comes after the mind with lies and the emotions with sinful feelings. This causes pain-filled responses that weaken the will and cause the soul to clamp down against the threat. Usually with fear, control and a host of coping strategies that many times result in soul triggers. He comes after the body through illnesses that also create responses that dominate the soul. If he has control of the soul and the body, the spirit cannot lead, and the Holy Spirit is automatically quenched and grieved. That is why God's prescription for not being led by the flesh is being led by the Spirit *(Gal. 5:16)*. No one can control their flesh with their flesh. That is only accomplished through the spirit controlled by the Holy Spirit.

Quenching words

Many quote the passage to not quench the Holy Spirit and then go on to come up with whatever they think quenches Him. We don't have to use our imaginations to come up with the answer of what quenches the Holy Spirit, it's contained in the context of that passage.

"Do not quench the Spirit; do not despise prophetic utterances."—*1 Thessalonians 5:19-20*

The original Greek, which is what the New Testament was primarily written in, did not contain punctuation. Interpreters added punctuation so that we could follow the original thought as best as they could determine. No period exists after the phrase "Do not quench the Spirit." The translators placed a semicolon after the phrase, meaning that the thought continues. In context, quenching the Spirit is done by despising prophetic utterances. The Greek word eksoutheneō translated "despising," means to count as nothing or treat with utter contempt or regard as lacking value.

The Greek word prophēteía translated "prophetic utterances," means divine predictions in about half the passages in which that word appears. The other half of the time it means sharing the mind of God in a particular situation. I give you all of this technical background to prove that quenching the Holy Spirit is specifically the activity of treating words from the Holy Spirit as having no value. It's ignoring what the Holy Spirit is saying to you. It is cultural for us to value what we think or what some well-educated person says over what the Holy Spirit is saying to your spirit. That is a recipe for staying wounded and blocked from hearing the voice of God your whole life. You will be led by your mind and therefore your soul, instead of your spirit.

Stay wounded, and even if you do hear from the Holy Spirit, it will be distorted by the idols or strongholds in the heart that are coping with the wounds of the heart.

"Therefore speak to them and tell them, 'Thus says the Lord God, "Any man of the house of Israel who sets up his idols in his heart, puts right before his face the stumbling block of his iniquity, and then comes to the prophet, I the Lord will be brought to give him an answer in the matter in view of the multitude of his idols." —Ezekiel 14:4*

God speaks through idols

This passage in Ezekiel says that if we have pain-avoiding strongholds (idols) in our hearts when we inquire of God, He will speak to us through the idols. In other words, His word will be distorted by the lens we are wearing which is colored by our strongholds. We will bend what He says to fit our desire to stay trapped in the stronghold, and we won't even know we are doing it. This is of course if we inquire of Him at all when we are in pain-avoiding patterns. This quenches the Spirit of God because it renders His voice to be utterly valueless.

For Jesus to be invited in to heal a memory, we will have to hear His voice without quenching it. Surrender our stronghold idols in the process, and our ability to listen to his voice will skyrocket. When someone is having difficulty hearing the Lord I will take them through all the unforgiveness in their hearts. I watch as the blocks get removed and it is like someone pulls the cotton out of their ears. They start hearing the voice of God through thoughts and visions on an amplified level.

Jesus knows no limits

Jesus, being outside of space and time, can bring total healing to events from our past. His omnipresence always reveals that He was there at the time of the painful incident that let in the core lie. Sometimes just seeing Him in the midst of the painful memory starts to bring healing to the wounded part of the heart that has been held captive at this moment in time.

Since we have already covered the idea that God is not controlling everything while being in control at the same time, we are not going to go back over all of it again. But in that moment of revisiting a painful memory where we see Jesus there, on occasion, the person will ask, "Then why didn't He stop it?" God has chosen to limit His sovereignty, for the most part, to function through His body here on the Earth. In other words, He is not in heaven throwing lightning bolts down at every injustice. When real people fail to protect those assigned to them, real people get hurt, even though Jesus was there in their midst. Amazing parents can take their eyes off their children for a minute, and abuse can happen.

Lie-based pain

A large part of the pain held in a memory does not come from the trauma itself. It comes from the lies we started believing about ourselves, and God as a result of the wound (as we saw in Pattern 2). Usually, only one memory contains the core lie or a pattern of memories. Other painful memories produce splinter lies that come from the core lie that, on occasion, Jesus will want to heal. But dealing with the core lie and its memory usually severely weakens the other memories if not makes them go away altogether. I have prayed with several people who either had a memory go completely away, or have lost all of their pain from the memory once Jesus heals them.

Many times when the lies are reconciled with the truth in a memory, all the pain goes away. This is consistent with the discovery that Type A trauma is harder to heal than Type B. Type A trauma is brought about by not receiving something you need, and Type B is brought about by abuse. In fact, part of the deception from the enemy is the belief that I can blame how my life turned out based on an event from my past. The enemy loves to get us to live out of a victim-heart posture. This is not to minimize the pain and trauma that do occur as the result of abuse, which need to be released to Jesus.

The most significant issues that prevent us from moving forward are lies that got implanted in the heart as a result of the trauma. Jesus comes to heal the whole thing, the trauma, and the lies. He is the only one that heals wounds as summed up in Isaiah 61 and He is the only one that can bring the light of the truth to expose the lies.

Time doesn't heal wounds

Many believe the myth that time heals wounds. I have watched Jesus heal wounds of the soul and then physical healing come once the spiritual healing takes place, but I have yet to see time heal a wound. I have seen people numb, stuff, block and rationalize memories thinking the injury is healed because they can't feel pain associated with the memory. Yet they wonder why they are full of fear, anger and a host of other issues. It's because they have hidden the hurt and not been healed from it. Until they are brave enough to let Jesus into the room of their soul/house where the memory is stored, the enemy will continue to use it to cause all kinds of triggers to control their behavior without them knowing the ultimate source.

I have seen a host of conditions healed right in front of me including PTSD, bipolar, schizophrenia, and Complex Regional Pain Syndrome. All four of these conditions, including others are said to be incurable by the medical community which is, of course, a correct assessment when you leave Jesus out of the treatment plan.

No forgiveness, no freedom

All four of those conditions included forgiveness and if we ever want to live in freedom, we cannot harbor any unforgiveness in our heart toward anyone. I start most of my sessions by leading people through forgiving those who have wounded their heart and therefore, according to Matthew 18, taken on a debt with them. There are a few reasons why I start there. Unforgiveness is the number one way demons gain access to our hearts. When unforgiveness is removed, a person gets unblocked in order to hear the voice of God more clearly. This is 100% a result of forgiveness. Everyone I have ever prayed with, after they forgive everyone they are led to forgive, have their spiritual hearing, sight and senses increase dramatically. Walking through forgiveness with yourself or someone else is a great way to get a quick snapshot of people's lives and the lies they are believing and how demons may have gained access to their hearts.

Most people I pray with do not understand the grace gift of forgiveness and its purpose. Matthew 18 is the template I use to understand and explain forgiveness. Forgiveness is frequently misunderstood as "letting the other person off the hook." I have even had people try to use that language in a session. However, forgiveness is a grace gift, from God, for the wounded person. It can also affect offenders when they experience the grace of God through an encounter with the one who forgives them. God accomplishes two purposes through forgiveness, but I believe the primary beneficiary is the person who has been hurt.

Without this gift of grace, we carry the offense the rest of our lives. Jesus paid a high price so we don't have to carry the heavy weight of that offense around with us. In the last half of Matthew 18, Jesus answers a question from Peter about how often he should forgive. Jesus responds with "70 times 7," which is a Jewish phrase that means infinity. In other words, you always have to forgive if you want to walk in the Father's freedom.

Jesus then tells Peter a parable about a servant that owes his master the equivalent of about 30 million dollars in today's money. No way could this servant pay it back, so the master ordered his wife, his kid, and the servant to be sold to get back some of the money. The slave begged the master, and the master wiped out the full 30 million that the slave owed him. That slave then found someone who owed him about 1,000 dollars in today's money and grabbed him by the throat and threw him in jail until he paid him every penny. The master heard about it and had the slave imprisoned, and the tormentors came until he paid back what he owed. Jesus tells the disciples that their Heavenly Father will do the same to them if they don't forgive their brother from their hearts. This is not a salvation passage – he is answering Peter's question about how often he had to forgive his brother. It is a quality of life issue. When we harbor unforgiveness in our hearts, we lock ourselves in a jail cell with the offense, and demonic cell-mates, and give them permission to torment us.

I then tell them these conclusions about forgiveness and unforgiveness.

Forgiveness

- Forgiveness is not a head issue; it is a matter of the heart. People often think they have forgiven, but really haven't in their hearts because the Holy Spirit will bring up the same person who they think they have forgiven.

- Forgiveness does not take into account the intent of the offender. It doesn't matter if the offender intended to harm or not; it doesn't even matter if they really didn't do anything wrong. It's about the offended releasing the offender from the debt or hurt or perceived debt or hurt in their heart.

- Forgiveness does not imply a relationship. You don't have to be in relationship to forgive.

- Forgiveness is about the offended releasing a debt owed to the offended by the offender.

Unforgiveness

- Unforgiveness locks the offended in a jail cell with the part of the offender they have not forgiven. They will eventually become the very thing they hate in the other person if they don't forgive.

- Unforgiveness gives the tormentors access to their souls. Demons gain access to us through unforgiveness as clearly stated in the parable.

- Unforgiveness that lingers turns into bitterness, bitterness that lingers turns into judgment. Judgment then becomes a worse offense than unforgiveness.

A favorite story of mine about how unforgiveness can be hidden in the heart and how it blocks our ability to hear the voice of God is with Calvin. As I led him through prayer we asked for the Holy Spirit to put on his mind anyone he needed to forgive. He did not hear anything, but in the Spirit, I immediately heard his dad. When I said, "I heard your dad," he said, "Shoot, I thought I had forgiven him for trying to kill me." Many times because we have mouthed the words I forgive—fill in the blank—we think we have forgiven the person, yet we still have hard feelings towards the person in our hearts. Forgiveness is a heart issue and not just mouthing the words. That is why we ask the Holy Spirit to reveal to the person if there is anyone they need to forgive.

Only He can reveal what is really going on in the heart of a person. I led him through forgiveness and then prayed again; "Holy Spirit, would you put anyone Calvin needs to forgive on his mind right now?" I heard the name, John. I asked him what he heard, and he said, "Nothing." I told him that I heard the name John and he said, "Shoot, I thought I had forgiven him. He tried to kill me too." I led him through forgiveness and then prayed again, Holy Spirit would you put anyone Calvin needs to forgive on his mind right now? I heard the name, Sally. I asked him what he heard, and he said, "Nothing." I told him that I heard the name Sally and he said, "Shoot, I thought I had forgiven her. She's my ex-girlfriend." I led him through forgiveness and all of a sudden he started hearing and seeing on an incredible level. He had an amazing session, and it revealed the power of unforgiveness to block our ability to clearly see and hear the voice of God.

Who God is to us in Pattern 7: **Jehovah-Rapha = The Lord that Heals**
Jeremiah calls for the faithless sons to return and Jehovah will "Rapha" or heal their faithlessness *(Jer. 3:22).* Encountering the God that heals demolishes faithlessness. He is the Lord we encounter when He heals the memories that have caused parts of our hearts to be in faithless bondage for much of our lives. Jehovah-Rapha heals not only the wounds and lies of the soul but those of the physical body as well. Physical healing is frequently the by-product when emotional wounds are healed and demons evicted.

The Lord that heals answers the question; "How can I love God with a whole heart when I only have a piece of a heart to give?" He answers with the miraculous gift of healing. He is the Lord that came to bind up the brokenhearted spoken of in Isaiah 61. He is Jesus. When we grab hold of the hem of His garment, the power to heal flows right out of Him and straight into the place in us that needs healing. Wholehearted people have a whole heart to give to the one who healed them. That one is Jehovah-Rapha, The Lord that heals.

Scripture: "Who pardons all your iniquities; who heals all your diseases; Who redeems your life from the pit; Who crowns you with loving kindness and compassion." —Psalm 103:3-4

Tool: Forgiveness and memory tool

Activation:
- Ask Jesus to show you everyone you need to forgive and what for.
- Deal with each person, one at a time, by saying "Father, I choose to forgive _____."
- Tear up each issue as a debt the person owes you and hand it to the Father.
- Ask what He gives you in return. (Many times whatever He gives in is what the person is seeking in that relationship.)
- If any forgiveness feels extra painful, ask Jesus if there is a memory associated with that person or circumstance that He wants to heal.
- Let Him heal each memory, one at a time.
- Write it down so you will know how you are trying to cope with life apart from Jesus. Repent of every strategy and stronghold and surrender them to Jesus and ask Him to take away the desire to self-protect and self-medicate.

Pattern 8:

Walking out His words

We are now free, and God is free to bless us to live out the words of the womb.

Joseph's Pattern 8: Now, nothing is restricting the blessing and favor of God flowing from heaven through his clean pipeline and into Joseph's life. He is fully functioning in his gifts and call. Dead to self, honoring his gifts and living out who God originally designed him to be, Joseph now experiences all that God has for him. He lives 110 years. Since he entered his world-leader role at age thirty, he experienced seventy plus years living out what Jesus called the abundant life. It says that he had a grandkid born on each knee which means he not only influenced those he ruled over, but the ripple effect of his life also trickled down through his generational lines. It even affected the Hebrew people to the point that they took his bones into the Promised Land as a testimony to God's faithfulness. And his life still resonates today as a testimony almost 4,000 years later.

"But Joseph said to them, 'Do not be afraid, for am I in God's place?' As for you, you meant evil against me, but God meant it for good in order to bring about this present result, to preserve many people alive." ...

"Now Joseph stayed in Egypt, he and his father's household, and Joseph lived one hundred and ten years. Joseph saw the third generation of Ephraim's sons; also the sons of Machir, the son of Manasseh, were born on Joseph's knees. Joseph said to his brothers, 'I am about to die, but God will surely take care of you and bring you up from this land to the land which He promised on oath to Abraham, to Isaac, and to Jacob.' Then Joseph made the sons of Israel swear, saying, 'God will surely take care of you, and you shall carry my bones up from here." — *Genesis 50:19, 22-25*

Joseph's destiny: Joseph lived out the fullness of his destiny, gifts, and calling that God had for his life, and it changed human history.

Joseph's legacy: Joseph left a legacy not only for his people but his life is a living testimony, thousands of years later to millions of people. His life story demonstrates how eagerly God wants to redeem every attack in our lives from the enemy. Looking through spiritual eyes, his story brings clarity to our story.

I'm pretty sure you have been able to relate most of these eight patterns to your life as you progressed through this take on Joseph's story. I'm also pretty sure you realized that your life is not as neat and orderly as the way the Joseph story is presented in Scripture. That's why I named these patterns and not steps. We can't just hold up the Joseph story as a template that we all march through life too in the same manner. I named these patterns and not steps because this is a journey and not a task to be accomplished. You can't try and run through the first seven patterns like an obstacle course so that you can get to the reward at the end of the story as quickly as possible.

Know patterns no formulas

These eight patterns represent real life. It seems to me that we are always in at least one of them and there are times when we seem to be in multiple patterns simultaneously. Another reason these are patterns is that they uniquely apply to each individual. There is no cookie cutter formula, but there are patterns. I have never witnessed anyone successfully put an individual or God in a predictable box. Life is not predictable, but life has seasons and patterns that we need to recognize, so we know where we are in the time clock of our lives. It's the conclusion Solomon reached when he penned the phrase, *"There is an appointed time for everything. And there is a time for every event under heaven." —Ecclesiastes 3:1*

Every farmer knows the four seasons he or she must recognize in order to make their living as a farmer. There are a lot of variations within these patterns, depending on many factors; what part of the world you live in, what crop you are growing, what pests there are in your location, how much fertilizer you need, what is the soil type, etc. There is no way to have a template that works for every farmer in every location in the world. But there are patterns, and if they are not heeded, failure will result. Even in the most basic farming terms, if you don't know you plant in the spring and harvest in the fall and you don't know how to tell when it's spring and when it's fall you'd better find another profession.

God has given us patterns to let us see seasons but not formulas. These eight patterns enable us to recognize seasons but how each person's life fits in these patterns will be as unique as their fingerprint or DNA. Without the Holy Spirit guiding us, we will be left with our reason or intellect, and we will try to force it and figure it out. Our intellect will want to run algorithms to predict the steps to accomplish instead of listening to the Holy Spirit tell us the pattern we are in and what He wants to say to us about it.

Mazes, cheese, and heart conditions
In the midst of all this discovery, God gave me a vision that I was sharing with a man over a meal. He was in a real pit. Circumstances

were pressing his face into the mud at the bottom of it, and he was not real happy with God about it. He had been there for years, even decades. At the time I was meeting with him there seemed to be no relief in sight from his perspective. I know better than to give advice in these situations since I quit taking my own advice about ten years ago. I now just surround myself with people who hear from God clearly. We ask His advice, and I go with the answers I get from Him directly, confirmed through others.

So my response to his frustrated tirade that morning toward God was to tell him about the vision I had seen a couple of days prior. I said "Brad, God showed me a vision a couple of days ago and it was straightforward. It was a maze with cheese at the end of the maze." I then told brad what God said to me: "Ray, everyone wants the cheese, but I don't care anything about the cheese; what I care about is the maze because in the maze I get to lock arms with them and walk through the maze together as I capture their hearts. Then, by the time we get to the cheese they can enjoy it without it destroying them. It won't own them and become an idol to them the way that it would have if I would have answered their original prayer and taken them straight to it. By the time we get to the cheese through the path of the maze, I can bless them with cheese of every kind and in unlimited supply. That's because they won't get their value from how much and what quality of cheese they have and they won't compare their cheese to other people's cheese to assess how they measure up in my plan. They will just be able to enjoy it as a blessing and a gift from me."

I watched this revelation sail right over Brad's head without so much as an eyebrow lift of acknowledgment that I had even said anything. It seemed like he was just preparing his next tirade against how unfair God was. What I was saying was delaying his dissertation on how bad his life was and how sound his theological reason was as to why God was treating him this way. I then said "Brad, it's like this, You want results, God wants your heart." I watched as the anointing on those words hit him in the chest like a mule kick. He visibly recoiled and mumbled, "Ok, I get it." The tirade stopped, and something shifted in him that day. Anointed words carry power. Anointed words only come by listening to the Holy Spirit. Anointed words come from the heart, not just the head.

Multiple pits and multiple shovels

Brad was just struggling with what we all wrestle with; the recognition that we may have multiple shovels and pits to work through on our way to rule over the Egypt assigned to us. We have to understand that we are not going to get a military escort from Jesus to go right past the pit and the prison, and straight to the throne of Egypt. The people of the Exodus generation didn't run straight into the Promised Land either.

You don't have to

But they also didn't have to wander in the desert for 40 years, griping and complaining and dying in the desert without ever making it to the Promised Land as most of them did. The presence of God can be just as profound in the wilderness as it is in the Promised Land. It's His presence we want to become addicted to, not the milk and honey of the Promised Land. The milk and honey are the cheese at the end of the maze. The maze is where we learn to recognize and crave the presence of Jesus. The cheese will taste even better after the long journey, and after the presence of Jesus has cleansed your palate so there is a heightened awareness and appreciation for the cheese.

Prosperity not puffery

Pattern 8 is certainly not the promise of a get rich quick scheme to motivate you to master the patterns for the purpose of receiving your mansion filled with sunshine, roses, and butterflies. But it is also not an excuse to over-react to the "God is a genie" theology. Don't allow prosperity formula preaching to cause you to put on a "life is tough brother" lens that squashes any positive assessment of hope in life of legitimate prosperity. That hammer of religious skepticism and overcorrection always misses the mark just as much as the place the correction started from.

The truth is that favor, blessing, and prosperity are part of the family inheritance from your Father. You just can't game the system to get it. To deny the fact that favor and blessing flow from the Father is to deny a large portion of scripture and a vital understanding of the love of the Father. Unfortunately, it is the place that a large part of Christianity has parked their cars of destiny in an attempt at correcting the deception of the get rich quick schemes from questionable leaders. *"Beloved, I pray that in all respects you may prosper and be in good health, just as your soul prospers." — 3 John 1:2*

Surrender attracts blessing

The real truth is that when we fully surrender in the pit, break agreement with the core lie and coping strategies, and live from a heart posture of forgiveness and generosity, our pipeline to heaven will remain clean and open. This will cause blessings to flow through it to us like oil. Jesus says that in this world you will have tribulation, but the good news is He doesn't stop there as most over-correction does. He continues His statement to say, "Take heart because I have overcome the world." Partnering with Him makes you an overcomer, not an over-compensator. In fact, when we fully surrender to Him, He promises to take care of us.

"But seek first His kingdom and His righteousness, and all these things will be added to you." —Matthew 6:33

Dangerous blessings

No doubt this place of blessing can be a dangerous place if you are not fully established in the value Jesus has placed on your life. Many have lost their way in Pattern 8. This is the place where you have to make sure your value gets settled in Jesus. Your value is the price love is willing to pay for you; it's what you are worth. There will always be a risk, while we are in this body, to get our value from things we can see, smell, taste, and touch. Because of this, prosperity seems like a very challenging test that few survive. Tangible expressions of worth or value in the natural realm look like real temptations to exchange for the true value that comes to us in the spiritual realm which resides in the heart.

Who are you

When God first sent me down the path of understanding our value, I thought it was just another way of expressing identity. I would say we can't get our value or identity from what we do. I thought value was a more precise word to show a way for us to stay out of performing to get our identity.

I had heard for years that our identity can only be found in Christ. But I was never really sure I knew exactly what that meant. There was still too much in those explanations left open for interpretation. Most of what I have heard focuses on Jesus living through me, my dying to self, and claiming all the positive things Jesus and the Father say about me; all the Scripture statements that express who I am in Jesus. Thank God for the people who teach about identity in Christ and that teaching was indeed a helpful part of my journey It helped establish some beautiful truths in my heart, but that language never really settled the bigger issue for me, and I wasn't really sure why. I wasn't sure I even knew what that bigger issue was.

What you do doesn't affect your value

It seemed like I started wrestling that bigger issue to the ground when I started coming to terms with the fact that I can't get my value from what I do. My value is what I am worth, what I cost, it's the price tag that love is willing to pay for me. Where I get my value seemed to be more of the issue than who I am and what my function is, which is what identity meant to me. Most of the teaching on identity will tell you that you can't get your identity from what you do. The problem is that part of identity is what you do. That's what made it so confusing for me. Paul spends a portion of 1 Corinthians 12 connecting your identity to where you fit in the body.

"For the body is not one member, but many. If the foot says, Because I am not a hand, I am not a part of the body," it is not, for this reason, any the less a part of the body. And if the ear says, "Because I am not an eye, I am not a part of the body," it is not, for this reason, any the less a part of the body."—1 Corinthians 12:14-16

Identity answers the belonging question

Identity settles the need for belonging. It's the second highest need that all humans have, but it is not the first in the order of priority. I spent years in the identity in Christ teaching trying not to get my "feel good" from what I do and was always a little uncertain and confused. The reason for me is that I believe identity is what you do, it's where you belong: I'm an eye, or I'm a foot, I'm a pastor, I'm a warrior, etc. Names have meaning in the Old Testament, and they have everything to do with the unique kind of life, gifts, and function of that individual throughout their earthly sojourn and, indeed, included what they did or were going to do. It seems that in our efforts to help us not connect performance to love we have redefined identity in a way that has made it confusing, at least to me.

Value is separate from identity

Then one day God spoke to me out of the blue when I wasn't even thinking about it and said; "Value is separate from identity." A cascade of thoughts hit me instantaneously as revelation built on top of revelation and what I had been wrestling with started to make sense to me for the first time.

I started connecting this concept to a reality that I already knew about the human condition. The number one need in this life is love and the second one is belonging. I then realized that value is the visible expression of love and identity is the visible expression of belonging. Value is how I know that I am loved, and identity is how I know I belong.

Value sets identity free

He showed me that if I know my value, it will free me not to get my value from my identity and that will allow me to walk fully and freely in my identity and destiny. If I try to get my value from my identity, it will pervert it into performance. The reason the enemy attacks and wounds our identity and gifting is to get us to try to prove our value from what we do.

If we let love give us value and let identity create belonging, we will securely attach to Jesus and have a healthy soul submitted to our spirit. We never want to try to secure love through identity. Neither do we ignore identity just because we have love. Both are core human needs that if they are not met, deep wounding will occur. We just want to make sure we receive them in the right order. This sounds harmless and maybe even correct to us on the surface, but if you dig a little deeper, you will discover that trying to get love from identity will cause us to perform to get love. That is a perversion of what can only be received by grace. If I try to devalue identity in an effort to avoid getting my value from it, I will not know what my purpose and gifts are and where I fit in.

As we learn our value to God, we start to come into alignment with love because of the deep interconnection between the two. "For God so loved the world, that He gave His only begotten Son." Whatever we bring under the reign and rule of Jesus has to obey His Kingdom authority. As we bring our value and our identity under the reign and rule of Jesus, healing, freedom, identity, value, and purpose start to flourish. If we understand, on a heart level, the value God placed on and in us by the price that He was willing to pay for us, we gain revelation into the intensity of God's love for us. Our need for value from another source goes away. If we understand our identity in Jesus which includes our destiny, call, and gifts, we will realize that we belong, that the Father has a place for us in His house. We will quit trying to fit in and know that we already do fit in. We will start looking for the place to plant and grow instead of the place to find acceptance.

David vs. Saul

It's interesting to compare David's journey into destiny with Saul's journey. The Father spoke value and love into David while he was tending sheep before his identity was realized. Saul went straight into identity without value being established first, and he failed the test in the end. These two lives are also living examples of the Old and New Covenants. The Old Covenant is based on externals and behaviors, while the New Covenant is based on values in the heart. The New Covenant is based on a new heart that is established in the value and love of the Father through Jesus. The Old Covenant is based on keeping an external code to find belonging or have an identity in what we do.

Saul looked good on the outside

Saul looked impressive on the outside. He was a head taller than any other man in Israel. He was the perfect candidate for the king since Israel had rejected God's rule over them and wanted a man; a king like all the other nations surrounding them. He was an impressive looking king, from the outside. Again, this is a perfect picture of law and grace. The Old Covenant or law makes demands on how you look to the outside world (a king ruling over Israel like the other nations). The new covenant is concerned with the heart and compares to a theocracy or God ruling over Israel. This indicates someone ruling over us who can't be seen on the outside. A theocracy would not be visible to the other nations, just as the New Covenant, where King Jesus rules over our heart, is not a law or visible code that rules over us. It's a love-versus-law motivation for living a righteous life.

David looked good on the inside

When God chose David, He told Samuel, "Man looks at the outward appearance, but the Lord looks at the heart" *(1 Sam. 6:7)*. David had a heart connected to God and established in the love and value of the Father. Saul's heart was insecure based on a devalued identity, as he looked at the externals of which tribe he came from.

Value before identity

The Father had already established love's value in David's heart while he tended sheep at the same place where he killed the lion and the bear. This was long before David ever walked in his identity as a king. Value was established before identity was realized and that was and still is a recipe for a man after God's own heart.

Saul, on the other hand, did not receive value before he received his identity as a king. When Samuel first encountered Saul and spoke identity over him by declaring him as God's anointed king over Israel, Saul responded out of his mouth what had been fermenting for years in his heart. The words were based on his core lie and declared;

"Am I not a Benjamite, of the smallest of the tribes of Israel, and my family the least of all the families of the tribe of Benjamin? Why then do you speak to me in this way?" —1 Samuel 9:21

When the insecurity from a core lie blames a lack of identity as the culprit for a devalued soul; it's the moment when identity begins being crafted as an idol in the heart. Trying to find belonging without love being first established as a foundation creates an idol-making factory in the deepest parts of our souls. Value is focused on whose you are; identity is focused on who you are. Value is worth, identity is function, Value tells me how much I am loved, identity tells me how I belong. Value teaches me how to rest; identity teaches me what to do.

Look at the contrast in David's statements when identity was challenged after value was established in his heart first.

"Who is this uncircumcised Philistine, that he should taunt the armies of the living God?" —1 Samuel 17:26

Identity minus value equals bondage

When value gets established, identity becomes bold and unapologetic because the possessor of it intimately knows the one who gives them value. Seeking identity apart from value being established, makes identity vulnerable to the level of demonic pressure the person is under at any given moment. Value-established identity will look like pride to the one who isn't established in value. This is especially true for someone who is dominated by a religious spirit. You will look a little too free, peaceful, and bold to fit their religiously inspired grid. You will be shining a light in the dark pit of their core lie. Insecure religious people will do everything they can to pull you back into the pit of your own core lie because their spiritual eyes are not used to that kind of radiant light. Your boldness is like a cattle prod to their insecurity. David's brother Eliab demonstrated this kind of reaction right after David asked the question, "Who is this uncircumcised Philistine?"

"Now Eliab his oldest brother heard when he spoke to the men; and Eliab's anger burned against David and he said, 'Why have you come down? And with whom have you left those few sheep in the wilderness? I know your insolence and the wickedness of your heart; for you have come down in order to see the battle.' But David said, 'What have I done now? Was it not just a question?" —1 Samuel 17:28-29

Saul's identity as king was disconnected from his value from God which is why he was so vulnerable to being a slave to the people. The enemy had Saul's core lie playing in a loop over and over again in his head, and sometimes that internal civil war manifested right out in the open. We attract activity in the spiritual realm like a magnet to bring to pass whatever we believe about ourselves in our hearts. Look at what some of the people said out loud after Samuel publicly declared Saul as King. This was of course, right after Saul had been found hiding among the supplies before his own announcement as King. *"But some rebels said, 'How can this man save us?' So they despised him and brought him no presents. But he held his peace." —1 Samuel 10:27*

How many times do you think the enemy replayed "How can this man save us?" over in Saul's head? How many times do you think the enemy reinforced his core lie by replaying the embarrassing youtube video, in his mind, of how he had to be coaxed out of hiding among the supplies to be announced as king. I speculate that Saul's core lie was "I'm not enough," and I can promise you that those two incidents were devastating, repeated, condemning bullets to the head of the newly-appointed King. Saul demonstrated how this core lie created the stronghold of people pleasing by letting the people keep the spoils of war after God had explicitly told him not to. It cost him his sanity, kingship, and eventually his life. It also caused a demonic spirit to attach to that stronghold which David managed for him by playing music that would temporarily make it stop manifesting *(1 Sam. 16:14-23).*

Saul also demonstrated his focus on identity as the solution to life by trying to get David to walk in his armor (externals/identity of a king). David rejected the identity (armor) of the king and chose the place he found value as a son with just a sling before his enemy. When you are armed with value, you are more dangerous than a nuclear warhead to the enemy. David sat at the table of value when his enemies came after him. He is the one that penned the words in Psalm 23, "You prepare a table before me in the presence of my enemies." David rested in the love and value of the Father when his identity was threatened.

Saul was focused on identity before value was ever established in his heart. He was anointed king without knowing he was loved and he couldn't handle it. The law focuses on the externals, but the one operating under it doesn't know they are loved and it becomes just about right and wrong without connection to relationship.

Jesus answers all the questions

Jesus is another beautiful example of value before identity. If you remember, after Jesus' baptism, the Father spoke audibly from heaven, "This is my beloved Son in whom I am well pleased" *(Matt. 3:17)*. Jesus hadn't even done anything yet. No miracles had been performed at that moment. I know some of you are saying that sonship is identity. I want to split hairs with you a little bit first, not to win an argument but to let you know where I am coming from. He had value first. The Father said He was beloved before He called Him a Son. He also reestablished value in the same sentence by saying He was well pleased with Him before Jesus had started performing as a son.

If you're a son, prove it

Jesus walked out of the Jordan, where He was baptized, and into the wilderness for forty days of testing and fasting, where the enemy went right after identity. The enemy knew he couldn't go after value, he had heard the audible voice of the Father as well. He had to go after identity. Just look at how the enemy tempted Jesus. He went right after sonship. The enemy was saying to Him, "Your value only comes from proving sonship. If you're a son prove it."

- *Prove it with your gifts as a son* (turn these stones into bread)
- *Prove it with your importance as a son* (jump off the temple and angels won't let you fall)
- *Prove it with your destiny as a son* (I'll give you a shortcut to the kingdom)

Because Jesus received value from the Father first, He was able to pass the identity test. After this testing, Scripture says He then walked in power, and He walked right into the synagogue in Nazareth and claimed His identity without apology from Isaiah 61. If you know you are loved and valued, you can boldly declare your identity without fear. The enemy won't be able to pervert it. He then went out and walked in His identity, gifting, and destiny, radically demonstrated the Kingdom and radically changed the world.

He taught it to the seventy

Jesus revealed this concept of separating identity from value to the seventy that He sent out to do the works of the Kingdom by healing and performing miracles. They are more than fired up when they returned. *"The seventy returned with joy, saying, 'Lord, even the demons are subject to us in Your name.' And He said to them, 'I was watching Satan fall from heaven like lightning. Behold, I have given you authority to tread on serpents and scorpions, and over all the power of the enemy, and nothing will injure you. Nevertheless do not rejoice in this, that the spirits are subject to you, but rejoice that your names are recorded in heaven."' —Luke 10:17-20*

The seventy said to Jesus "Even the demons are subject to us in Your name." He high-fived them and said, "Way to go, you guys are killing it out there! I even saw Mr. Big get knocked off his perch. Satan gets his bragging rights blasted out of Heaven because you're bringing the Kingdom to Earth through healing, deliverance, and all the visible supernatural demonstrations of the Kingdom. Keep doing it; don't stop. However, don't get your value from it. Don't get your value from your identity, what you do, how you belong and whether you fit in. Get it from the price I paid for you to have a permanent place of connection with me in Heaven."

In fact, to prove it, your name is written in the lambs' book of life and can't be removed. Even if next week you chicken out and refuse to go out again and do the work of the Kingdom, it won't affect your value because your name will always be in the book. It's because your value, your worth, and your price tag have been paid, and it's a settled issue with Me. You have been bought with my blood even before it was shed *(Rev. 13:8)*.

Righteous revelation

At this point it is important we address one more issue that we dug deeply into in Pattern 6 that needs to be placed between value and identity. It seems to be connective tissue between the two and that is the reality of righteousness. Neither value nor identity completely settle the need to be in righteous, right standing before the Father. We have an eternal need to be righteous. Some recognize this and have placed it in the identity bucket and I am okay with that. But I think it is really an issue that needs deeper exploration outside of identity even though I can make the case that it is part of our identity in Jesus.

When we get hit with the heart revelation that we are righteous in our spirit, we will understand and live out of true value and identity. We will actually be able to freely receive the value and identity that are ours in Jesus through righteousness. It is the umbilical cord that connects value and identity together and attaches them to Jesus. It will allow us to, as the author of Hebrews puts it, "boldly come before the throne of grace and find help in time of need." Righteousness is such a key component to living free that additional boldness and freedom will break out in our heart through righteousness even if we have settled value in our hearts and walk in our identity. Righteousness will be the jet fuel poured on the fire already burning hot after living from a place of value and identity in Jesus. Righteousness is the Jesus injected reality that helps kill the performance virus in our souls.

No more value

You never have to live a performance-based life. You never have to live in that unstable place of believing that when you perform miracles, you have more value than when you don't. Don't rejoice, and don't tie your value to what you do or who you are, get your value from who's you are. Jesus said "You are mine, and I bought and paid for you. Now get out there and keep killing it, you are amazing. Run with boldness and freedom, and Satan will fall like lighting."

The table prepared before your enemies

There's a tool God has given me to help establish value in the hearts of those I pray with that I call the table of value. It has become a very effective tool to displace the core lie in our hearts with the truth of the value that Jesus has placed on each of our lives. It is an interactive way to meet with Jesus and let him reveal the truth about the high price He paid for each one of us. This tool helps truth land in our hearts and not just our heads. Every core lie the enemy puts in our hearts is to devalue us so that we will seek value from everything else, even what we accomplish, instead of the price of love that Jesus paid. I share an activation at the end of this pattern to teach you how to use this tool.

Overview of the table

We ask Jesus to meet us at the table of value. Everything that appears in the vision at the table has meaning. It reveals that we are trying to get some of our value from anyone who shows up in the vision. If other people are there, we give Jesus permission to ask them to leave because no one else establishes your value except Jesus. We have to know that the table of value is where Jesus shows us our value. No one else gets a seat at that table. Our spouses, our children, our boss, our friends do not get a seat at that table. Only you and Jesus get to sit at that table. Nothing else establishes our value or worth except Him. We then stay in the encounter and let Jesus pour value and love into us in the place.

"You prepare a table before me in the presence of my enemies;
You have anointed my head with oil;
My cup overflows." —Psalm 23:5

Notice the order. The table of value comes first, and it is established right in the enemy's face, then the anointing of identity comes next. When both of these come from the Lord and in the right order, my soul's cup overflows with gladness, and it will cause the rest of Psalm 23 to happen as goodness and loving kindness will follow me around all the days of my life. This heart posture will cause me to dwell, or stay in the presence of Jesus every day of my life, no matter what my enemies are doing and this will be a dress rehearsal for what's going to happen in me for all of eternity. Sign me up!

Value can't be renegotiated

An analogy of the table of value can be made with buying a car. The dealer cashes our check and hands us the title. Is the value of the car now a settled issue? We can't go back a week later and try to renegotiate the value of the vehicle after the fact. Just realize that the enemy has been getting us to go back and re-negotiate our value with every devaluing event of our life. Our value is a settled issue. Jesus finalized it 2,000 years ago. It cannot be re-negotiated no matter what we are going through. Jesus didn't even ask your permission before He paid your price in full. As Romans 5:8 says He did it while we were yet sinners. He didn't even ask anything from us to establish our value and worth to Him by dying on the cross when we had no value. He saw the gold inside of us that the Father placed in our hearts in the womb and He said to the Father, "I'll die for that joy you just set before me." You are the joy that was set before Him, and you cost Him everything.

My time at the table

I have had amazing encounters with Jesus at the table of value myself. When I went to the table and met Jesus there, I noticed the top of my table was all scarred and beaten and He told me it represented all the wounds and pain that I had been through. I then saw my name carved into the top of the table, and that triggered a memory of when I was attending a very religious school when I was young: I was carving my name into the top of a desk. The teacher caught me, took me outside the classroom, and whipped me for destroying property. Jesus asked me if I knew why I had done that and I replied, "No." He said, "You were trying to find your identity in that place that was devaluing you with religion. You didn't know me yet, and you didn't know how to find out the value I had placed on your life, because they were trying to get you to earn it instead of receiving it. You were just crying out for some kind of belonging or identity."

He then stood up and poured gold nuggets all over the top of the table of value and started to wave his hand over the top of the gold. I noticed a hot, blue flame coming out from under His hand, and it melted the gold as it ran down and filled in all of the scars and deep cuts on the table top. I knew this was a picture of how valuable I was to Him and how he turned everything the enemy meant for evil into gold, and I wept. While the gold was still soft, He grabbed my hands and pressed them down into to it to make an impression and a resting place for my hands for future encounters with Him at the table. That table was mine: It had my prints, and I belonged there, and no one else did. I then noticed the gold started to cover my hands and run through my veins and arteries and up into my heart. As He looked at me with blue flames for eyes, it ignited my arms as blue flames flickered up and down both my arms, and liquid gold was dripping off of me in gold flame drops that fell onto the floor. I was undone.

I return to this vision when I am laying hands on people to pray for them because it keeps my heart focused on Jesus and not what I am doing. The power of the Holy Spirit and the love of Jesus flow through me like that liquid gold that coursed through my veins that day.

Rapid deployment

We can rapidly accelerate into our gifting, destiny and call by removing the roadblocks that prevent us from doing so.

Anton is someone that I prayed with at a facility that helps addicted people find freedom in Jesus with my spiritual son, Craig. Anton was first on the list of 6 guys we were praying with that day and it was the first time I had prayed at that facility. When he walked into the room and sat down he was looking all over the room and saying whatever came into his mind without a filter. He said, "I am bipolar, schizophrenic and I am not on my meds." I thought, no kidding. I asked the Holy Spirit what I was supposed to do since I couldn't really communicate with him in a way that would lead to inner healing.

I heard the Holy Spirit say to me, "Just start getting the spirits off of him." Craig and I started doing just straight deliverance with no inner healing and did so for about an hour and a half, getting rid of all the spirits that were identified.

We then laid hands on him and broke the diagnosis of bipolar/schizophrenia and commanded healing in Jesus' name. All of a sudden he opened his eyes and for the first time looked me in the eyes. I thought, something just happened. We had to move to our next session and prayed for five more guys that day. That night out on the porch of that house, Anton came up to Craig and me and said, "You guys did what eight years of therapy and seven years of drugs couldn't do. I am healed of bipolar/schizophrenia." I was blown away but wanted to make sure it was true before I said anything. Craig mentors the guys at that facility and called me the next week and said, "Anton is healed of bipolar/schizophrenia." I went back out with Craig a few weeks later to do the inner healing part since I don't like deliverance without inner/healing, and Anton was very powerfully touched by the Holy Spirit as even more freedom came.

I saw prophetically what he was going to be doing, and it was so amazing that I struggled for words. All that I could come up with to describe what I was seeing was to call him a "spiritual savant." I said "You are going to be like a five-year-old playing Mozart." And that is exactly what has happened to him. I have never witnessed a transformation like his nor have I seen anyone take advantage of what the Lord has done the way he did. He has an understanding of the spiritual realm that few I have ever met do. He moves in healing and the prophetic on a level that leaves me shaking my head and he is less than a year in the Lord. Rapid destiny happens to hungry surrendered hearts.

You cost Him everything

You are so valuable to the Father that you cost Jesus everything. You are the joy that was set before Him that made the cross worth it for Jesus. You are the treasure the man Jesus found and buried in the field called planet Earth. He went back and sold everything He had to buy the treasure. He then stepped out of heaven and into an earth suit and crawled up on a cross and left everything He had on that hill. That allowed him to buy the whole field of planet Earth and win all authority over it just so He could get you. You are the treasure, the joy, and the pearl of great price!

Nobody like you has ever existed or ever will again. Your identity, gifts, destiny, and call on your life make you as spiritually unique as your physical DNA or your fingerprint. There is a unique call on your life that started the second the Father spoke over you and breathed life into your cells as an embryo in your mother's womb. You were born out of value and richly adorned with a God-given identity. All of creation is waiting on its manifestation.

"For the anxious longing of the creation waits eagerly for the revealing of the sons of God." —Romans 8:19

The only things not unique about you are these eight patterns that I believe are common to everyone who has ever or will ever exist. This should give you hope in a God who wants to take the very attack that the enemy thought would destroy you and use that very attack to defeat the enemy with. We can see God doing this very thing throughout scripture.

The biggest stick of all that God has used to beat the devil with is the cross. Satan thought he had a master plan to get the very people Jesus came to establish the Kingdom of God on Earth through, the Jewish people, and inspired them to cry out for the death of Jesus. I just imagine him celebrating his victory while Jesus is giving up His spirit on the cross. When Jesus cried out the words "It is finished," Satan had no idea those words actually applied to him as well. Those words were spoken at the height of the most arrogant point in all of Satan's existence. Three days later that stick of humiliation Jesus hung on crushed the head of Satan as predicted in *Genesis 3:15*. It was with the cross that Jesus beat the devil with his own stick.

Who God is to us in Pattern 8: **El Shaddai = Lord God Almighty**

Jacob encountered El Shaddai after He changed Jacob's name to Israel. He declared Himself to be God Almighty as He proceeded to prophesy blessing and favor over Jacob's life. It is in Pattern 8 that we encounter El Shaddai as He prophesies over us blessing and favor and reconnects us to the words of the womb. Shaddai is believed to be derived from the Hebrew word for "breast" and from another word that means "strength and power."

El Shaddai nourishes and blesses the needs of those who surrender to Him like a mother to her children, and at the same time with strength and power. The tender heart of the Father and the powerful strength of His hand sustains us in a place of favor and blessing. It's the table where we sit with Jesus, and all our enemies can do is watch how all their attacks have driven us right into the arms of El Shaddai. It's underneath that table where God uses our feet to crush the head of the snake *(Rom. 16:20)*. It's the place where God takes the stick the enemy has been beating us with away from him and hands it to us and says, "Now it's your turn."

Scripture: "You prepare a table before me in the presence of my enemies; You have anointed my head with oil; My cup overflows." —Psalm 23:5

Tool: The table of value

Activation:
• Ask Jesus if He will meet you at the table of value. Write down everything you see.
• Based on what you see, diagnose with Jesus if you are getting your value from anything or anyone else besides Jesus. If you are, repent and give Jesus permission to remove from the table, the persons or things that have become idols to you.
• You cannot get your value from anyone or anything besides Jesus. Interact with Jesus about the things in the vision that are supposed to be there. What are the meanings or symbols of different things Jesus is showing you about His value and appreciation of you.
• Ask Jesus what your value is to Him.
• Ask Jesus if you can meet Him there anytime you want.
• Go there every day and every time you feel triggered to get your value from something or someone other than Jesus.

Conclusion:

You are free to move about the Kingdom.

An unexamined life will always result in an unremarkable life.

1. Fix your eyes on Jesus.

The ultimate weapon in spiritual warfare is to be so focused on Jesus that the enemy cannot get to you or distract you. Real freedom is not the absence of demons, it's the presence of Jesus. Meet with Him daily and sit in His presence, with worship, or the secret place, or the table of value, or with Bible study revelation, or with journaling, or with recording and interpreting your dreams. Stay focused on Jesus, and the devil will be really uncomfortable around you. Meditate on Him and speak over yourself the prophetic words you have received, especially the words of the womb.

2. Know the gospel and understand righteousness.

Understand what it means that you've been made a new creation. Core to the enemy's strategy is to make you think you are who you were before you received Jesus. He doesn't like who you are or your future, so he will reach into the past and try to bring you back to your old self. His number one strategy is to make you think you are that old corpse that Jesus crucified *(see Romans 6)*. When temptation comes, it is the enemy speaking to you. Evil desires are rooted in the enemy, they are not rooted in you. You are a new creation. Many who need deliverance are under condemnation from the enemy, which causes them not to like themselves.

3. Live under grace and not law.

Law is one of the key weapons the enemy uses to condemn us. Many who need deliverance are usually very heavy under the law or a performance-based relationship with God. They will even try and earn their deliverance just like they try and earn God's approval for everything else.

"Having canceled out the certificate of debt consisting of decrees against us, which was hostile to us; and He has taken it out of the way, having nailed it to the cross. When He had disarmed the rulers and authorities, He made a public display of them, having triumphed over them through Him." — *Colossians 2:14-15*

4. Know that value answers the biggest need in your heart which is love.

You have to be established in the value that Jesus has placed on your life. The number one need of the human race is love and value is the visible demonstration of the price that love was willing to pay for you. You cost Jesus everything.

"But God demonstrates His own love toward us in that while we were yet sinners Christ died for us.". — *Romans 5:8*

Go to the table of value and let Jesus reestablish His value for your life. Encountering Jesus changes your perception of your value.

5. Know that identity answers the second biggest need in your heart which is belonging.

Your identity is who you are and what you do. It's the words God prophesied over you in the womb. It defines you. You're an eye, or you're a foot. When love is established in your heart through value, you will not try to get your value from your identity (who you are or what you do), and it will free you up to run.

"Therefore, since we have so great a cloud of witnesses surrounding us, let us also lay aside every encumbrance and the sin which so easily entangles us, and let us run with endurance the race that is set before us, fixing our eyes on Jesus, the author and perfecter of faith." —Hebrews 12:1-2b

The encumbrances are the core lies, and generational iniquities that are weighing you down and the sin is the pain avoiding strongholds that result. Let value lift off the lies and cover the sin so you can run in your true identity without the gifts and call being perverted into value seeking entanglements. We can then fix our eyes on Jesus who births faith in us and causes hypomonē (Jesus endurance) to rise up in us so that we can run the race all the way to the finish line.

Ask Jesus to reveal the words prophesied over you in the womb. Write them down. Speak them over yourself on a regular basis. These words are your identity.

6. Know what the core lies are that the enemy placed in your heart.
There is a lie about you, a lie about Jesus, and a lie about the Father. Know how they interconnect in a web over your head to keep you in the pit. You don't focus on them, but you have to always know the lies he put in your heart at an early age because he will never get off that topic. Most of the attacks that will come your way will have some upward link to the strategy of the core lie. Know the core lies the enemy put in your heart about Jesus and the Father. They will be strategically linked to the core lie about you.

7. Have a no tolerance policy for the strongholds you use to protect from the core lie.
Most of the demonic strongholds in your life are a result of coping with the core lies the enemy put in your heart. He has programmed you through years of training to respond to your core lie getting poked to trigger into a stronghold partnered with a spirit. As soon as you find yourself there repent of the activity and break agreement with any spirits that have attached and command them to go in Jesus

name. Meet with Jesus till your peace comes back and your value is reestablished in your heart. Speak your identity in Jesus out loud and move on.

8. Learn the difference between an atmosphere and a demonic attachment.

As your discernment gift increases, you will be more and more aware of atmospheres you encounter as well as sensitivity to demonic attachments on you. Many times they will feel the same but are drastically different issues.

Atmospheres are felt when you are picking up the predominate spirits in a location. Everything from homes to nations have atmospheres. Atmospheres, like attachments, are based on agreements. Atmospheres have multiple people in agreement with a spirit and attachments are agreements you have made with spirits that have allowed them to attach to you.

How to deal with attachments: Find out the spirit and break agreement with it and command it to go in Jesus name until you feel it lift. If it does not lift, there is still an agreement with it.

How to deal with atmospheres: Tell the spirit that they don't set the atmosphere, Jesus does. Tell anything coming into your atmosphere they have to submit to the Lordship of Jesus since everything in your life is submitted to His Lordship. Then ask the Holy Spirit to place a bubble of peace around you and carry it everywhere you go.

9. Live a surrendered lifestyle.

You will never walk in freedom until you fully surrender your life to Jesus. Anything short of unconditional surrender will cause you to be double-minded, and you will be unstable in all your ways. Any unsurrendered area of your life is an area you are protecting with your flesh and will be an open back door to the house of your soul. Spirts will have free rein to come and go through that open door.

10. Know you are dead to sin and therefore free from sin.

You have to live in the reality of Romans 6 that you are free from sin in order to be free. When a sinful thought comes your way, know that it is not from you since you are dead to sin. Don't receive it, act on it, or let the enemy accuse you for having it. Replace it with the truth of righteousness.

11. Pray in the opposite spirit.

Whatever the enemy is saying to you, pray out loud in the opposite direction. If he is trying to get you to be angry with someone pray a blessing over them. If he is attacking, ask the father to turn every attack into a blessing for you. The heart of the father is ready to turn every attack into a blessing. You are asking him to do what he already wants to do, which is to turn your life into a Joseph story. He will only be able to do this as you posture your heart in faith and peace, knowing he can turn all things together for good for those who love him and are called according to his purpose *(Rom. 8:28)*.

12. Don't let the enemy make you feel guilty for hearing his voice.

The enemy will give you a thought and then accuse you of having it. *"The sheep follow him because they know his voice. A stranger they simply will not follow, but will flee from him, because they do not know the voice of strangers."— John 10:4*

Jesus promises that you will not follow the voice not that you won't hear the voice of the enemy. There is nothing wrong with hearing the enemies' voice, just don't own the enemies' voice. It can't hurt you unless you come into agreement with it. This is about finding Jesus in the situation, not stopping the enemy from talking. When you can find Jesus in the situation, then He can take you out of it. The enemy will work to get you focused on the enemy instead of God.

13. Don't internalize the voice of the enemy.

The enemy wants to speak to us and have us think it is coming from us. When we think we are the source, we are one step away from condemnation. Because we are righteous, when what we hear is bad, it means it is coming from an outside source, not from us. Our heart is good now because of righteousness. Don't own the enemies' thoughts. We have a new heart, and we are a new creation.

14. Don't try to live a spiritually unconscious life.

The day you received Jesus, you forfeited the right to a spiritually unconscious life. Many want a quick deliverance fix so they can say they have been delivered and go back to not having to think about or participate in the battle they are in.

15. Understand that freedom is a process.

Truth builds. A structure is being built. Line upon line precept upon precept is how freedom is built. All of us are in process. Be willing to walk that journey. When you are in pain, you want a quick fix. Most of the time it doesn't work that way. Celebrate the freedom you have and understand that everything in the kingdom is a seed and it grows.

MINING
THE TRUTH

Please visit our website at miningthetruth.com to purchase more books, sign up for our newsletter, sign up for training, or keep up with our calendar, and blog. Also be sure to like us on Facebook and follow us on Instagram. You can also contact us on the website to schedule Ray to speak, or train your organization.

NOTES

NOTES

NOTES

NOTES

NOTES